Boarding the Future

Governing Transformation from Boardroom to Startup

By Fabio Teixeira

Boarding the Future:
Governing Transformation from Boardroom to Startup

By Fabio Teixeira

For information, contact
BDI Publishers, Atlanta, Georgia
bdipublishers@gmail.com

BDI Publishers
BDI PUBLISHERS
Atlanta, Georgia

ISBN: 978-1-946637-49-9

CONTENTS

ACKNOWLEDGEMENTS

This book would not exist without the unwavering support of my wife and our two children. They not only encouraged me to write, but stood beside me through the many international chapters of my journey, sharing the fun, sacrifices, the uncertainty, and the growth that come with building a life across borders. Their patience, love, and belief in me made this work possible.

I am deeply grateful to my father and mother, whose example taught me resilience, humility, and the importance of never giving up, lessons that continue to guide both my leadership and my life. I also owe sincere thanks to my sisters, mentors, friends, teammates, and clients, who I've had the privilege to learn and be inspired from over the years. Every conversation, challenge, and collaboration shaped the thinking reflected in these pages. This book is as much a product of those shared experiences as it is of my own.

INTRODUCTION

Are you ready for the governance of the future?

There are moments in history when the rules of leadership change faster than leaders can adapt. We are living through one of them. When you sit in executive or board meetings today, have you noticed it? A slide on AI appears late in the agenda, labeled "technology update." A management team assures you the model is "working as intended," but no one can clearly explain its risks, its assumptions, or its limits. Decisions that once took quarters are now made in weeks, or days, yet the governance structures overseeing them still move at yesterday's pace. You feel the pressure to move faster, but also the unease that speed is outpacing understanding. The meeting adjourns, action items are assigned, and the room empties but the questions linger: Are we actually governing what matters most? Or are we reacting to forces we no longer fully control?

That unease is not imagined. AI is accelerating decisions at machine speed, startups are redefining expectations for velocity, and legacy institutions are straining under the weight of transformation. At the same time, geopolitics is redrawing markets and alliances, while trust, the currency that sustains every institution, has become more fragile than ever.

If you sit on a board, lead an organization, advise founders, or govern risk, you have likely felt this tension already. Meetings feel fuller, agendas longer, yet clarity harder to reach. Decisions arrive faster, but consequences linger longer. The questions are no longer theoretical; they are immediate, personal, and consequential.

Across boardrooms, startups, universities, and industry forums, I hear the same question echoed in different accents and contexts:

How do we lead in a world where everything is changing at once?

This book is my attempt to answer that question, not through abstract theory, but through three decades of executive, board, entrepreneur and advisory experience across global corporations, franchise operations, and technology & AI startups. And through what I have seen, repeatedly, one truth stands out:

Leadership today is not about choosing between the old world and the new one. It's about learning to bridge them.

Legacy industries teach us discipline, safety, resilience, and stewardship. Startups teach us agility, experimentation, ingenuity, and customer obsession. AI demands foresight, ethics, speed, and bold governance. Global complexity requires humility, adaptability, and cultural intelligence. And the next generation demands authenticity, purpose, and transparency.

The leaders who will thrive in the next decade, board members, founders, executives, and emerging leaders, will be those who can combine these worlds without becoming trapped by any single one of them.

Who This Book Is For

If you're reading this, chances are you don't need another book telling you how boards work or what leadership *should* look like. You've been in the room. You've made hard calls with imperfect information. You've lived through transformations that looked clean on slides, but were messy in reality.

This book is not written to lecture you. It's written to challenge you.

It's for leaders who feel the weight of a rapidly shifting world and sense that the old governance playbooks, while once effective, are no longer enough on their own. It's for those moments when you leave a board or executive meeting with a quiet question lingering in your mind: Are we truly governing what matters now, or are we relying on structures designed for a different era?

This book is for you if you are:

- A board director navigating AI, risk, ethics, and transformation at scale

- A startup founder building fast and wondering how much governance is enough and when

- An executive leading complex change locally or across borders

- An investor or advisor focused on resilience, accountability, and long-term value

- An operator trying to connect innovation with discipline, speed with trust

- Or a next-generation leader preparing to step into governance roles with intention

Whether you've served on boards for decades or are joining your first advisory board, this book meets you where you are. The cases span startups, legacy companies, global enterprises, and moments of crisis and reinvention, not to prescribe answers, but to surface better questions.

In fact, some of the most valuable parts of this book are not the frameworks or examples, but the reflection questions woven through every chapter. They're designed to make you pause mid-read, challenge assumptions, and spark conversations at the board table, in offsites, or in your own thinking. Strong board members are not only defined by how much they know but they are also defined by how willing they are to keep learning.

If you believe that good governance is never finished, that leadership requires continuous self-examination, and that the best boards evolve by questioning themselves before the world forces them to—this book is for you.

Not to tell you what to think, but to help you think more clearly about what comes next.

What This Book Will Help You Do

Across these chapters, you won't find a single "right" model of governance—and you don't need one. You already bring experience, judgment, and context to the table. What this book is designed to give you is something subtler, and ultimately more useful: the ability to pressure-test your own governance model against a world that has changed faster than most boards have.

The most valuable moments in this book are not the frameworks or cases on their own, it's what happens when you pause at the reflection questions and ask, "How does this show up in our company, our board, our startup, right now?" Those questions are not meant to produce perfect answers. They're meant to surface blind spots, challenge assumptions, and help you decide what to strengthen, what to simplify, and what no longer fits.

You don't need to adopt every tool or replicate every example. No two organizations face the same risks, cultures, or constraints. Instead, you'll encounter multiple governance patterns, drawn from startups, legacy industries, global companies, and boardrooms under pressure, and use them as comparative lenses. The reflection questions help you validate what you already do well, identify where your governance is outdated, and adjust your approach to better match the realities of AI, speed, global complexity, and trust.

The core outcome of this book is practical judgment, the kind that allows leaders to balance agility with discipline, govern technology without pretending to be technical, and evolve boards and leadership systems without overengineering them.

By engaging with the questions individually, as a board, or in leadership discussions, you'll be able to modernize your governance in a way that fits your organization, rather than forcing your organization to fit a borrowed model. This is not about learning governance from scratch; it's about learning how to keep it relevant.

In practical terms, this means shorter decision cycles, fewer governance failures, stronger investor confidence, more resilient operations, and organizations that grow with credibility instead of volatility. By reading this book and implementing its principles, governance becomes a source of competitive advantage because governance is no longer about protecting the past, it is about enabling the future. Boards must evolve from compliance monitors to stewards of trust and technology. Executives must evolve from operators to architects of adaptability. Founders must evolve from visionaries to system-builders. Leaders must evolve from controlling uncertainty to navigating it with courage, curiosity, and ingenuity.

By the end of this book, you will be able to answer questions that increasingly define success or failure in leadership today:

- *What must modern boards do differently to stay relevant?*
- *How do leaders balance speed with discipline without creating risk blind spots?*

- *How do we govern AI responsibly across borders, cultures, and regulatory regimes?*
- *How do we scale trust faster than technology?*
- *How do we lead with values that endure through crises, not just through growth?*

These are not theoretical questions. They are the ones investors, regulators, employees, customers, and markets are already asking sometimes explicitly, often implicitly.

You will see global cases where organizations succeeded because they adapted and others failed because they did not. But beyond tools, frameworks, and stories, you will learn something deeper:

The true purpose of governance today is not only to defend yesterday's decisions, but to create tomorrow's possibilities.

And by applying what you learn here, you will be able to make faster, higher-quality decisions without increasing risk, reduce costly governance failures before they surface publicly, improve investor confidence and stakeholder trust, and align strategy, talent, and accountability so transformation reaches customers, markets, and ultimately the bottom line.

In practical terms, this means shorter decision cycles, fewer surprises, stronger credibility, and organizations that grow with integrity instead of volatility. By reading this book and implementing its principles, governance becomes a competitive advantage because governance is no longer about protecting the past, it is about enabling the future.

How to Use This Book

This book is designed to meet you where you are.

You may read it sequentially, following the arc from entrepreneurial agility to global adaptability and the board of the future. Or you may read it non-linearly, engaging with the chapters most relevant to your current challenge—AI oversight, startup governance, resilience, global leadership, or board transformation.

Each chapter ends with reflection questions, and in my view, these may be the most valuable pages in the book. Don't skip them. If even a few of these questions spark deeper, more honest conversations in your boardroom, that alone is a win. As a board member myself, I use questions like these regularly—not as theory, but as a way to surface blind spots, challenge assumptions, and shift the quality of dialogue. While writing this book, I shared several of these questions with fellow directors and advisors, simply to see what would happen. The response was immediate: better conversations, sharper focus, and decisions grounded in what actually matters. These are not rhetorical prompts; they are practical tools you can use in board meetings, offsites, governance reviews, or quiet moments of personal reflection. They are meant to help you test what you already have in place, decide what needs to evolve, and lead with greater clarity in a world that rarely slows down.

The importance of agility for your convenience, the appendix compiles all reflection questions from every chapter in one place. Many readers return to this section repeatedly, before board evaluations, strategy offsites, or moments of inflection using it as a living governance checklist.

Why This Book, and Why Now?

The last few years have stripped away any illusion that governance, strategy, and leadership operate in stable conditions. A global pandemic shut down supply chains overnight. Geopolitical tensions reshaped energy markets, technology access, and capital flows. Wars, trade restrictions, sanctions, and industrial policy began influencing boardroom decisions as much as financial forecasts. At the same time, technology accelerated faster than most governance systems could absorb, AI moved from experimentation to decision-making, cyber risk became existential, and digital platforms scaled globally before regulators could respond. In this environment, agility is no longer a startup advantage, resilience is no longer a legacy strength, and governance can no longer be static. The leaders and boards who thrived through this period did not predict every shock, but they were prepared to adapt, decide, and learn faster than the disruption around them.

These forces are not abstract trends, they are already reshaping how decisions are made, how risk materializes, and why the traditional rules of leadership no longer apply. The next decade will not reward leaders who are merely experienced, it will expose those who are unprepared. The future will belong to leaders who can:

- Govern technology without hiding behind complexity
- Move at entrepreneurial speed without sacrificing accountability
- Balance global scale with local legitimacy
- Build trust as deliberately as they build growth

The risk of not developing these capabilities is no longer abstract. Boards that fail to evolve will miss opportunities they never see, approve strategies they do not fully understand, and react to crises they could have prevented. Organizations will lose market share not because their products failed, but because their governance lagged behind the pace of change. Trust will erode quietly through biased algorithms, misaligned incentives, cultural blind spots, and decisions that look defensible on paper but indefensible in public.

If you do not rethink how governance works now, someone else, regulators, activists, competitors, or markets will do it for you, under far less favorable conditions. This book exists to help you avoid that outcome. It gives you the frameworks, questions, and mindset needed to govern transformation with confidence before disruption forces your hand.

We are entering an era where AI can influence every decision, but values will determine every outcome.

Where transformation will define market winners, but resilience will determine who endures.

Where global fragmentation will challenge organizations, but adaptability will empower them.

The world does not need more leaders who know the answers. It needs leaders who ask better questions, learn faster, and lead with clarity in uncertainty.

A Reflection Before You Begin

Before turning the page, pause and ask yourself:

- *Are you leading for the world that was or the world that is emerging?*
- *Is your board or organization building adaptability intentionally or hoping for it?*
- *Do you see governance as a burden or as a strategic advantage?*
- *How prepared are you to govern in an age shaped by AI, geopolitics, and global interdependence?*
- *What leadership legacy are you actively shaping?*

If these questions resonate, this book is for you.

Now, let's begin the journey—
from oversight to stewardship,
from complexity to clarity,
from disruption to purpose-driven transformation.

Welcome to the future of governance.

Your leadership moment begins now.

Chapter 1

Built for One World. Responsible for Another.

Where Governance Came from and Where It Must Go Next

The message arrived just after midnight.

A global CEO, someone I had known for years, texted me five words that captured a moment every leader now understands:

"The system made the call."

Their company had just experienced an AI-driven operational failure. Not because someone broke a rule. Not because a team made a mistake. But because an algorithm, designed to optimize efficiency, had rerouted critical logistics without human review. Customers were furious, regulators were alert, and the board was blindsided.

Hours later, as the crisis unfolded, one director spoke quietly but with striking clarity: *"We built governance for a world that no longer exists."* That sentence has stayed with me ever since. It captured a realization that every director, sooner or later, is forced to confront—that the true risk was never the algorithm itself, but the governance surrounding it. And whether you sit on a global corporate board, advise a startup, run a franchise, or build a new venture from scratch, the same truth applies: leadership today is being tested not by technology alone, but by the governance and systems we designed to guide it.

The world changed faster than governance did:

- AI reshaped decisions.
- Startups rewrote speed.
- Geopolitics fractured markets.
- Workforces evolved across generations and cultures.
- Resilience became a daily test, not a distant concept.

Yet most governance systems, around the globe, were built for a slower, more predictable age.

Why Governance Must Evolve Now

If the last decade taught us anything, it is that governance in its traditional form cannot keep pace with modern disruption.

Markets now shift in days, not years. Algorithms influence decisions faster than leaders can react. Regulation moves globally, not locally. Startups can scale from garage to global in under five years. Legacy industries can collapse with one reputational failure.

And in all of this…

Boards that ignore AI governance risk irrelevance.
Boards that embrace it gain advantage.
Boards that resist agility get bypassed.
Boards that combine discipline and adaptability thrive.

But the real inflection point is this:

AI changed the nature of decisions. Therefore, it changed the nature of governance.

No board—corporate, startup, nonprofit, public, family-owned—can lead effectively without understanding:

- how AI creates risk and opportunity
- how culture scales across borders

- how resilience is designed, not improvised
- how startup speed can be integrated into legacy structures
- how servant leadership becomes the ultimate source of legitimacy

Governance is no longer a backward-looking function. It is a forward-looking capability. And Chapter 1 sets the stage for why your leadership and your board must evolve with urgency.

The Long Arc of Governance: How Boards Came to Be — and Why They Must Change Again

If governance feels strained, it is not because you or your board are failing. It is because you are governing a radically different world with tools designed for another era. Modern boards are being asked to oversee autonomous technologies, global ecosystems, cultural legitimacy, and machine-speed decisions using frameworks built to protect capital, monitor agents, and prevent fraud at a distance. The gap you feel is real, but it is structural, not a reflection of competence or commitment.

This history is not academic. It explains why good boards still fail, why experienced directors feel unprepared, why governance structures feel heavy yet ineffective, why AI incidents catch leadership by surprise, and why culture fractures during transformation. Boards were never designed to govern learning systems, invisible values embedded in code, or trust that can be lost globally in minutes. Understanding where governance came from is the first step toward evolving it. So, boards can stop reacting to complexity and start shaping it.

1600s–1800s | The Merchant Era — Protecting Capital at a Distance

Governance focus: Capital protection, agent oversight

Why boards existed: Investors funded ventures they could not see or control

Primary risks: Fraud, loss of cargo, misuse of funds

Board posture: Defensive, transactional

The earliest forms of governance emerged in the 16th and 17th centuries, when merchant ventures and joint-stock companies sent ships, capital, and authority far beyond the reach of their owners. Distance created uncertainty. Investors needed a way to oversee managers operating across oceans and months of silence. Governance became the mechanism that made trust possible when visibility was not.

Boards were designed to protect capital, monitor agents, enforce rules, and prevent abuse. Risk was tangible and immediate: ships sank, cargo vanished, and power was misused. Governance was defensive by design, focused on financial control and rule enforcement. That DNA still shapes modern boardrooms today, visible in audit committees, fiduciary duties, and the enduring obsession with financial reporting. It worked when the greatest threat was physical distance and slow information, but it assumed trust could be enforced by ownership alone, an assumption the modern world no longer allows.

1800s–1940s | The Industrial Era — Control, Scale, and Stability

Governance focus: Efficiency, safety, operational discipline

Why boards evolved: Factories, railroads, utilities required scale and reliability

Primary risks: Accidents, labor unrest, supply disruption

Board posture: Supervisory, compliance-driven

As industrialization surged through the 19th and early 20th centuries, governance evolved in form but not in spirit. Factories replaced ships, railroads replaced trade routes, and corporations grew larger, more centralized, and more complex. Boards expanded, committees formed, reporting cycles standardized, and accounting became the dominant language of oversight. Governance focused on capital allocation, operational efficiency, regulatory compliance, and predictable scale. This was the age of managerial capitalism, built on the assumption that professional managers knew best and boards existed to supervise execution rather than challenge strategy or culture.

That posture delivered stability and resilience. Risk committees, safety standards, and process discipline emerged as safeguards in industries where failure carried human and financial cost. But it was governance designed for machines and factories, not for ambiguity, rapid change, or autonomous systems. Innovation moved at human speed, markets evolved gradually, and governance fit its time. The problem is that much of this logic still governs boardrooms today long after the environment it was built for disappeared.

1950s–1990s | Managerial Capitalism — Oversight at Arm's Length

Governance focus: Monitoring professional managers

Why boards stabilized: Markets moved slowly, information was centralized

Primary risks: Agency problems, accounting manipulation

Board posture: Periodic, reactive

After World War II, corporations expanded across borders, but governance remained largely national, episodic, and static.

Boardrooms filled with former CEOs, bankers, lawyers, and industry veterans whose value lay in experience and reputation. Meetings were quarterly, sometimes biannual. Information flowed upward in dense, carefully curated packets. The board's posture was supervisory, not inquisitive. Success meant clean audits, steady dividends, regulatory compliance, and—above all—no scandals. For decades, this model worked because disruption moved slowly, reputational damage unfolded over years, and technology did not scale decisions faster than human judgment could intervene.

That world no longer exists. Many boards still operate with structures built for the industrial and postwar eras while governing organizations driven by algorithms, platforms, and global networks. The result is a widening mismatch: twentieth-century governance confronting real-time risk; financial literacy without technological fluency; compliance checklists without ethical foresight. This failure is not negligence, it is lag. Governance evolved incrementally while the world accelerated exponentially. AI did not break governance; it revealed its limits. Quarterly oversight cannot manage systems that decide in milliseconds, and passive supervision assumes management can fully explain systems that increasingly act beyond human intuition.

2000s | The Compliance Era — Financial Accountability

Governance focus: Transparency, internal controls

Trigger: Corporate scandals and financial fraud

Primary risks: Misreporting, governance failure

Board posture: Procedural, rule-based

The early 2000s delivered a reckoning for corporate governance.

Accounting scandals at Enron, WorldCom, and Tyco exposed profound failures in oversight and trust. The response was Sarbanes–Oxley, a sweeping reset that redefined expectations around internal controls, audit independence, and financial reporting. For financial governance, it worked. It restored confidence by addressing a clear threat: human manipulation of numbers. Markets needed discipline, and Sarbanes–Oxley delivered it.

But Sarbanes–Oxley solved yesterday's problem. It was never designed to prepare boards for algorithmic decision-making, data ethics, automation cascades, AI-driven discrimination, cyber risk at scale, or global digital regulation. Today's governance crisis is not about false numbers; it is about opaque systems making consequential decisions faster than boards can interrogate them. The tools directors rely on controls, audits, checklists were built to look backward, not to govern what is emerging. Sarbanes–Oxley restored financial trust, but it left boards exposed to the new frontier of risk: technology that acts, learns, and scales beyond traditional oversight.

2010s–Present | The Digital & AI Era — Governing Autonomous Systems

Governance focus: Ethics, accountability, trust at scale

Why governance is stressed: Algorithms decide faster than humans

Primary risks: Bias, opacity, automation cascades, reputational collapse

Board posture required: Active, literate, anticipatory

Every major evolution in governance has been triggered by

a shift in how risk manifests. Trade created distance risk. Industrialization introduced scale risk. Financialization exposed transparency risk. AI introduces something fundamentally different: autonomy risk. For the first time, boards are governing systems that learn without explicit instruction, change behavior over time, act faster than humans can supervise, embed values invisibly, and scale mistakes globally. This is not an incremental shift, it is a categorical one, and it demands a governance response of equal magnitude.

The questions boards must now ask are different at their core: *What does the system optimize for? Who is accountable when it fails? Can we explain this decision publicly to a regulator, a customer, or a headline?* Boards have mastered governance for capital, scale, and compliance, but they were never designed for autonomy, algorithms, and acceleration. Today, directors are not only governing decisions; they are governing decision-making systems themselves. That requires a new design discipline—one capable of keeping pace with technology, global complexity, and the realities of autonomous action.

Now–Future | The Global Stewardship Era — Trust Across Borders

Governance focus: Legitimacy, agility, adaptability, long-term value

Why boards must evolve again: AI, geopolitics, global regulation, cultural divergence

Primary risks: Loss of trust, regulatory fracture, social backlash

Board posture required: Stewardship, learning, legitimacy

Startups quietly changed the tempo of governance. While

corporate boards debated control, startups operated with no luxury of perfect information, endless capital, or layered approvals. They governed through clear ownership, fast feedback loops, continuous learning, and extreme accountability. This was not chaos; it was disciplined speed. What startups revealed, often unintentionally, is that effective governance does not slow decisions; it clarifies responsibility. The lesson for modern boards is not to become startups, but to deliberately import startup agility into governance design, so speed and accountability reinforce rather than undermine each other.

At the same time, legacy industries preserved something equally critical: institutional resilience. Energy, aviation, utilities, and manufacturing amongst others learned, often through hard experience, that redundancy saves lives, discipline prevents catastrophe, scenario planning is non-negotiable, and culture determines outcomes under stress. These sectors endured because governance was embedded into operations, not layered on top as an afterthought. The future of governance is not startup speed alone; it is speed anchored in discipline, the marriage of adaptability with rigor.

Globalization completed the transformation. Boards no longer govern within national borders but across legal regimes, cultural interpretations of trust, geopolitical tensions, and data sovereignty laws. A decision approved unanimously in one country can trigger regulatory action, consumer backlash, or political scrutiny elsewhere. This reality pushes governance beyond approval into interpretation. Across centuries, boards evolved to protect capital, control behavior, and prevent failure. The next evolution adds a new mandate: enabling trust at scale with customers, employees, regulators, communities, and investors. That is why the board's role is shifting from oversight to stewardship, from control to guidance, from compliance to legitimacy, and from experience alone to continuous learning.

The purpose of this chapter and this book is to help you evolve governance consciously, rather than reactively. To understand:

- What must be preserved
- What must be redesigned
- What must be learned anew

Because governance has always evolved in response to the world and the world just changed again. The history of governance shows us one thing clearly: boards do not fail because they lack intelligence or integrity. They fail because they govern the future with structures built for the past. The chapters that follow are about redesigning governance for the world now unfolding and for the one arriving faster than most leaders expect.

A World Where Everything Moves Faster Than Governance

AI is no longer a technology conversation. It is a governance conversation. Algorithms now influence who gets hired, who gets credit, how prices are set, which content is amplified, and how operations respond in real time. These systems do not just execute instructions; they learn, adapt, and scale decisions faster than any management team can intervene. In doing so, they quietly encode values about fairness, efficiency, risk, and profit and then apply them at machine speed. Whether those values are intentional or accidental is no longer a technical question. It is a board-level responsibility.

Yet in many organizations, AI still appears late in the agenda, framed as a systems upgrade or an efficiency tool, delegated to the CIO or CTO, and discussed primarily in terms of cost, performance, or competitive advantage. The governance questions, accountability, explainability, bias, resilience, and trust, are often implied rather than examined. Boards assume that if the technology is working, the governance must be as well. That assumption is increasingly dangerous. When AI fails, it does not fail quietly. It fails at scale, in public, and often across borders, turning operational issues into reputational, regulatory, and strategic crises overnight.

This widening gap between technological speed and governance readiness is the defining leadership challenge of our time. Decisions that once unfolded over months now cascade in seconds. Risks that once remained local now travel globally. Oversight structures designed for quarterly review are being asked to govern systems that evolve continuously. This is not a call for boards to become technologists, but it is a call for them to evolve how they govern. The chapters that follow are built around this reality: governance must move faster and not by reacting impulsively, but by becoming more adaptive, more intentional, and more fit for a world where technology no longer waits for permission

Startups changed the rules of speed

Startups changed the rules of speed. Legacy industries debated for months what startups executed in weeks. Operating under extreme constraints, limited capital, limited time, limited people, startups learned to make decisions without perfect information. Scarcity became a forcing function. It clarified priorities, shortened feedback loops, and pushed accountability to the edges of the organization. Speed was not a cultural preference; it was a survival requirement.

By contrast, large organizations operate in an environment of abundance. There are more resources, more stakeholders, more reputational risk, and more layers of approval. This creates caution by design. Decisions are tested, stress-tested, reviewed, and optimized before action. That discipline has value, it prevents reckless moves and protects scale, but it also introduces friction. When markets moved slowly, this model worked. When technology and customer expectations now move at startup speed, it increasingly fails.

The future of governance cannot choose between these worlds. It must bridge them. The discipline of legacy industries provides resilience, safety, and trust. The agility of startups provides learning velocity, responsiveness, and relevance. Boards that lean too far in either direction break the system, either by suffocating innovation or by accelerating without guardrails. The chapters ahead explore how modern governance blends both: importing startup speed into decision-making while anchoring it in the discipline required to scale responsibly.

Global complexity reshaped risk

Global complexity reshaped risk but what makes this moment unique is how abruptly the context has shifted. For decades, many boards governed during one of the longest periods of relative geopolitical stability in modern history. Globalization expanded, supply chains optimized, capital flowed freely, and cross-border growth was largely framed as an opportunity rather than a vulnerability. Risk felt containable. Disruption was episodic. Governance models quietly assumed continuity.

That assumption no longer holds. In just a few years, boards have been forced to confront a very different world, one marked by trade wars, real wars, sanctions regimes, tariff shocks, and rising nationalism. Ukraine. Gaza. Venezuela. Taiwan. Iran. Red Sea shipping routes. Energy security. Data sovereignty. These are no longer abstract headlines; they are board-level variables with immediate operational consequences. A decision that feels safe in Houston may violate regulations in Hamburg. A data practice acceptable in California could be illegal in São Paulo. A partnership that works in Singapore might trigger national-security scrutiny in Washington or Brussels. What once looked like execution risk is now geopolitical exposure.

Many directors can point to a specific moment when this shift became undeniable. For some, it was a supplier suddenly cut off by sanctions. For others, a market exit forced overnight by regulatory change. Or a board debate about whether continuing operations in a region was a moral decision, a legal one, or both. These are the conversations boards are now having behind closed doors: *How exposed are we to geopolitical shock? How fast could we unwind or reconfigure operations? Who inside the organization is scanning these risks before they hit our P&L? How do we make a call when there is no clearly "right" answer and only trade-offs?*

This is why the "home-country mindset" and status quo no longer works. Boards must now lead with global awareness, cross-border intelligence, geopolitical sensitivity, and cultural fluency, not as soft skills, but as governance capabilities. Oversight today requires interpretation as much as approval. The chapters that follow will explore how boards build this muscle: how they anticipate global disruption rather than react to it, how they prepare organizations for shocks they cannot predict, and how governance evolves when the world itself becomes the most volatile risk factor of all.

Resilience became a daily operating requirement.

Resilience became a daily operating requirement. During the COVID-19 pandemic, we learned, painfully that resilience is not something you improvise in a crisis; it is a capability you build long before you need it. Overnight, boards were forced to confront questions they had never rehearsed at scale: *How long can we operate if supply chains break? What happens if entire regions shut down? How do we protect people, liquidity, and trust simultaneously?* The organizations that weathered the shock were not necessarily the most innovative, they were the ones with governance systems sturdy enough to absorb stress without collapsing.

Legacy industries survived because they were built on discipline spending decades institutionalizing safety margins, redundancy, scenario planning, and operational rigor. Their governance structures assumed failure was possible and prepared for it. When disruption hit, they did not panic; they executed. Discipline created endurance. But discipline alone was not enough. In many cases, slow decision cycles and rigid processes struggled to keep pace with a crisis that evolved by the hour.

Startups survived because they were built on adaptability. With limited capital, small teams, and no legacy systems to protect, they pivoted rapidly reconfiguring offerings, shifting channels, and rewriting operating models in weeks, sometimes days. Their governance was lean, informal, and tightly coupled to learning. They did not wait for perfect data; they moved, adjusted, and moved again. Adaptability created speed. But adaptability without structure also exposed fragility, burning teams out or amplifying risk when decisions scaled too quickly.

The future belongs to leaders who master both. Resilience in the next decade will not come from discipline *or* adaptability, it will come from their integration. The chapters ahead explore how boards and leaders design governance systems that absorb shock *and* evolve under pressure, how they borrow resilience from legacy industries without inheriting rigidity, and how they adopt startup agility without sacrificing accountability. In a world where disruption is no longer an exception but the operating environment, resilience becomes not a response but a standing capability.

Closing Reflection

As you start your book journey and reflections, ask yourself:

Which era of governance does your board most resemble today and which risks does that leave ungoverned?

Where are algorithms, platforms, or automated systems already making decisions faster than your board reviews them?

Does your governance model prioritize learning, or does it reward certainty and precedent?

Where is your organization relying on resilience it hopes it has, rather than resilience it has designed?

If a major AI or reputational incident occurred tomorrow, would your board know who is accountable within hours or days?

What decisions in your organization are already being made without meaningful human oversight?

Which risks are invisible to your current governance structure?

Are you governing for the past or for the systems now shaping your future?

Chapter 2

Entrepreneurship Agility from the Ground Up: Startup Lessons for the Boardroom

The Shock of Speed

When you move from a global corporate boardroom into the world of entrepreneurship and startup incubation, you don't just change your address, you cross into another universe. In the corporate world, executives debate billion-dollar projects for months before signing a single decision. Risk committees dissect scenarios, consultants flood inboxes with reports, and endless drafts circle between departments. By the time a strategy gets approved, sometimes, the market has already shifted, leaving well-intentioned plans running behind.

In the startup world, three founders huddle in a co-working space and pivot their business model before lunch. They launch a new feature in the afternoon, test it with real users, and by evening, decide whether to double down or discard it. There are no committees, no consultants, no waiting for approvals, just relentless experimentation. Every decision is a bet placed with limited time and capital. Success depends not on perfect plans but on speed, curiosity, and the courage to adapt faster than the market moves.

I have lived in both worlds. Large corporations taught me the value of discipline, risk management, and capital stewardship. Later, as an entrepreneur and small business owner running dozens of consumer-facing franchises, I experienced the immediacy of decisions that directly affected employees and customers. Staff shortage, a marketing error, or a single customer complaint could affect revenue tomorrow. Most recently, advising early-stage ventures has shown me the raw intensity of entrepreneurial speed, where survival depends not just on moving fast, but on learning faster and pivoting before competitors or regulators catch up.

In global corporations, leadership meant overseeing long-cycle projects, implementing safety systems, and navigating regulations. Decisions were large, complex, and deliberate. They demanded patience and precision. In franchising, leadership became visceral. Decisions were fast, local, and often emotional, visible in daily operations and in the faces of employees and customers. In startups, agility became existential. Success hinged on how quickly we could pivot, test, and respond to change. The pace was relentless, but it was also exhilarating.

This shock of speed is not just cultural, it is structural. Entrepreneurship is a laboratory for leadership under pressure. It forces assumptions to be stress-tested in real time. It demands a mindset, accountability, and courage at a pace legacy organizations often find uncomfortable. It is where "good enough today" can matter more than "perfect next month."

What these environments taught me is that agility is not recklessness, it is disciplined adaptability. The best entrepreneurs are not gamblers; they are architects of calculated risk. And the best boards are not bureaucrats; they are enablers of intelligent speed.

But here's the truth: today's boards and executives must import entrepreneurial agility into their governance if they want to survive disruption. So, ask yourself: *how long does it take for your board or leadership team to make a meaningful decision? Weeks? Months? Imagine competing against a startup that decides in hours.*

Could your team pivot that fast if the market changes tomorrow? How would you respond? If your company faces a sudden market shock tomorrow, could your leadership team pivot within days?

This chapter helps you bridge those two worlds. You'll see how entrepreneurial agility isn't chaos, it's disciplined adaptability that boards and executives can learn, structure, and scale. Through stories, boardroom reflections, and practical frameworks, you'll learn how to make faster decisions without losing accountability, how to build learning loops that strengthen strategy, and how to transform speed into a governance asset rather than a risk. By the end, you'll not only understand why startups move differently, you'll know how to apply those lessons to make your own organization faster, smarter, and more resilient.

Lessons Corporate Must Absorb

What surprised me most when I stepped from the corporate boardroom into the startup world was how quickly everything moved and how exposed that speed made every leader feel. In a global corporation, I was used to long meetings, risk reviews, and polished decks that took weeks to prepare before any real decision was made. In my first week advising a startup, I watched three founders sketch a business model on a whiteboard, debate for ten minutes, and pivot their entire product plan before lunch. No consultants, no committees, just conviction and adaptation to the market and voice of the customers. It was raw and unsettling but also exhilarating. Entrepreneurship, I realized, strips leadership to its essentials: adaptability, clarity, and courage. There's nowhere to hide behind process or hierarchy. You make a call, live with the consequences, and learn faster than comfort allows.

The real difference between startups and corporations isn't size, it's the speed of learning. Startups make ten decisions a day and refine their instincts; corporates spend ten days debating one and call it alignment. Yet I also came to see that both worlds hold truths the other needs. Startups must mature without losing agility, and corporates must rediscover how to move without fear. The leadership test isn't choosing between the two, it's designing systems that let discipline and speed coexist, where governance doesn't slow momentum but gives it direction.

Speed with Accountability

In the entrepreneurial world, speed is oxygen. Without it, ventures suffocate. Yet speed without accountability can create chaos, waste, or reputational disaster. The magic lies in blending rapid decision-making with disciplined verification.

Consider the story of a young payments' startup. The market it faced was dominated by slow, bureaucratic incumbents whose systems frustrated developers and merchants. Integrating with those systems could take weeks, sometimes months. The startup's founders took a different approach: they launched a simple, developer-friendly tool in a matter of weeks. They prioritized speed over perfection, releasing early versions that solved immediate pain points.

What they did differently was not only move fast but embed accountability loops from the beginning. Each release came with feedback requests. Developers were asked: "What works? What breaks? What must change? That constant cycle of launch-measure-adjust gave the company both speed and credibility.

The results were dramatic. Within five years, the company processed billions in global transactions. Its simplicity and speed attracted startups first, then enterprise clients. Eventually, even the incumbents were forced to adapt.

When was the last time your board or executive team approved a pilot project that launched in weeks, not years? Do you demand perfect plans before you act, or do you create accountability loops that allow you to act quickly and correct courses?

If your answers point toward caution, the solution is calibration, not speed for its own sake. Establish clear thresholds for experimentation and replace long approval chains with shorter, data-driven reviews that allow pilots to move forward responsibly. At the board level, make learning an explicit agenda item, ask management not only what succeeded, but what was learned and how that knowledge will scale. By defining guardrails instead of gates, and by framing agility as an expression of governance rather than a threat to it, boards can align pace with purpose. This is how you transform innovation from isolated activity into a disciplined, repeatable capability.

Speed without accountability is reckless. But speed with disciplined verification becomes a defensible strategy. Boards must insist on agility without losing control and that balance is the essence of governance in disruption.

Learning Loops

Failure isn't shame; it's feedback. Startups treat experiments as data, not disasters.

Failure has an almost mythical stigma in legacy corporations. Projects are managed to avoid embarrassment, not to maximize learning. Yet in entrepreneurship, failure is not a verdict, it is an input into the next decision. Every failed test is data. Every pivot is progress.

I often think of Airbnb's early story when I talk about agility and governance in the same sentence. The company began as a scrappy experiment which two founders renting out air mattresses during a San Francisco design conference to cover their rent. What started as a side hustle soon grew into a movement that challenged the very definition of hospitality. Yet from the beginning, it faced fierce resistance. Regulators dismissed it as unsafe; hotel associations fought it as unfair, and communities worried about neighborhood disruption. City by city, safety codes, zoning laws, and tax disputes piled up faster than listings.

What impressed me most was not their technology; it was their mindset. Rather than retreat under pressure, Airbnb's founders treated every city as a live experiment. When New York cracked down, they tested compliance models in Portland. When Paris demanded transparency, they built registration systems and began collecting taxes on behalf of hosts. When trust became the barrier, they introduced verification, reviews, and the now-famous host guarantee. Each confrontation became a feedback loop that strengthened, not weakened, the model.

That evolution offers a powerful lesson for boardrooms and leadership teams. Airbnb didn't win because it broke the rules, it won because it learned faster than regulators could say no. It turned governance friction into innovation fuel. For directors and executives, that's the real takeaway: agility isn't about avoiding resistance; it's about learning from it faster than your competitors. Governance, when done right, doesn't slow innovation, it teaches it how to survive.

Within a decade, that small platform was facilitating millions of stays across nearly 200 countries. It was far from smooth, bans, lawsuits, and crises followed, but its culture of learning loops allowed it to adapt faster than any competitor.

Now think about your own governance structures: *Would your board tolerate a failed pilot project as a step toward learning? Or would that failure be punished and buried? Do your executives know how to treat experiments as data, not disasters?*

The future belongs to leaders who normalize learning loops. Boards must stop equating failure with incompetence and instead measure how quickly organizations extract insight and apply it.

Adaptability in Scarcity

Scarcity is one of the most powerful things you can do to increase the creativity of your organization and grow it. Startups are born without the resources of multinationals. They lack brand recognition, capital reserves, or political influence. But scarcity sharpens focus and forces resourcefulness. Scarcity forces sharper focus, resourcefulness, and creative problem-solving.

In one of the clearest examples of adaptability born from scarcity, I often cite the story of a ride-sharing company that redefined what resilience looks like under constraint. Entering markets dominated by powerful taxi monopolies, it faced resistance on every front, tight regulations, legal challenges, and public skepticism about safety and legitimacy. I once spoke with a director who followed the company's evolution closely. "They weren't scaling with resources," he told me, "they were scaling with grit."

With little capital and no political backing, the founders had to innovate through necessity. They built a smartphone-based platform to connect riders and drivers, introduced dynamic pricing to manage demand spikes, and created a two-way rating system to enforce trust and accountability without adding cost. Each new city became an experiment in adaptation: in some, they partnered with regulators; in others, they rewrote the playbook entirely. Scarcity didn't slow them; it sharpened their judgment.

A decade later, the company had facilitated billions of rides across hundreds of cities. Its edge wasn't abundance; it was learning agility. It thrived because constraint became its operating principle, every obstacle a lesson, every setback a prototype for improvement. The takeaway for leaders and boards is timeless: when resources are scarce, adaptability becomes your strategy. Governance that thrives under constraint isn't reactive, it's experimental, disciplined, and relentlessly focused on what truly matters.

Scarcity can be a teacher for established corporations too. Abundant resources often hide inefficiencies. When money is easy, creativity stagnates. So, ask yourself: *What would your organization do differently if your budget were cut in half tomorrow? Would you collapse under the weight of lost resources, or would you focus on what truly creates value?*

As a board member, you can use scarcity as an opportunity to sharpen your choices and drive meaningful innovation.

Using Uncertainty to Increase Your Company Strength

Operating as though every day could be your last builds a mindset that thrives under disruption. Entrepreneurship also teaches leaders to live with existential risk. In a startup, uncertainty is not a season, it is the weather. Every day could be the last if funding dries up, a competitor launches faster, or regulations shift. Your ability to be flexible will allow your organization to stick around while others vanish in conditions of uncertainty. Strength under uncertainty is what separates ventures that survive from those that vanish.

Take the case of a young health-tech company trying to scale globally. It faced enormous uncertainty: fragmented regulations across countries, investor skepticism, and the constant risk of clinical trial setbacks. In this environment, nothing was predictable. Yet the company learned to operate as though uncertainty was permanent.

It diversified funding sources rather than relying on one investor. It created modular compliance systems so it could adapt to different regulatory regimes. It engaged customers early, even before products were fully mature, to build trust and iterate.

The result was flexibility. Despite repeated shocks, funding delays, trial failures, regulatory hurdles, the company scaled across multiple regions and became a trusted partner in digital health. Its strength was not eliminating uncertainty but building muscle to thrive within it.

For boards, this lesson is vital. Too often, corporate governance assumes stability. But in today's world, disruption is constant. *Is your board governing as if you have unlimited time and certainty? Or are you building systems that can withstand shocks, pivot under pressure, and sustain performance when the ground shifts beneath you?*

Strength under uncertainty is no longer optional, it is the baseline of leadership in the digital era.

The Agility Transfer Model for Boards

So how can boards and executives import entrepreneurial agility without losing the discipline that corporations require? I call this the **Agility Transfer Model**. It rests on five principles that capture the essence of entrepreneurial leadership while anchoring it in governance discipline.

1. Pilot & Pivot – The Discipline of Small Bets

Boards must encourage management to run small pilots rather than demand perfect plans. Pilots generate evidence; pivots keep organizations responsive. The governance role is not to slow decisions down but to ensure lessons are captured and scaled responsibly.

Startups live by this rule. They don't wait for certainty; they act, test, measure, and adjust. In contrast, many corporates waste months perfecting slide decks for projects that never launch. The pilot-and-pivot approach avoids paralysis by analysis.

This is what I call the "small bets" mindset: run bounded experiments with clear objectives, then decide whether to scale, pivot, or stop. A failed pilot isn't wasted—it is a source of insight that saves millions compared to a failed full-scale rollout.

Does your board allow management to place small bets, or do you demand certainty before action?

2. Customer Obsession – Beyond the End User

In startups, customers are not abstractions, they are lifelines. Without them, survival ends quickly. Boards must demand more than quarterly survey results. They should insist on mechanisms that bring customer voices directly into strategy, whether through advisory councils, real-time analytics, or even board-level customer sessions.

But "customer" can mean more than the end user. Keep in mind that your true customers may not be the end users. In some cases, they are the intermediaries to reach the end user such as franchisees in franchising systems, distributors in manufacturing, procurement officers in enterprise technology, or regulators in healthcare. If those stakeholders fail, the business fails, even if end consumers are happy.

Boards that understand this nuance help management focus not only on consumers but also on the broader ecosystem of stakeholders that determines success.

Does your board know who your real customers are and are their voices shaping decisions? When was the last time that your Board talked directly to some of the customers?

3. Cash Discipline – Liquidity as Oxygen

Startups know one truth better than anyone: liquidity is oxygen. You can have a great idea, loyal customers, and a promising market, but without cash you suffocate.

Corporations, flush with capital, often forget this. Yet in every crisis, financial downturns, pandemics, supply shocks, cash determines who survives and who fails. Boards should therefore prioritize cash reserves and liquidity buffers as much as profit margins. Liquidity enables agility when disruption hits.

Importantly, cash discipline cannot be left to the CFO alone. Every employee should understand how their daily actions affect cash flow. When people at every level see the link between their choices and liquidity, they become active guardians of strength.

Does your organization treat cash as a strategic enabler or as an afterthought?

4. Accountability Loops – Speed Without Bureaucracy

Fast decisions must still be verifiable. Boards should require mid-project milestones, checkpoints, and reviews, not to stifle speed, but to build trust that agility is disciplined.

This does not mean adding bureaucratic reporting layers. In fact, heavy processes kill the agility that boards are trying to enable. Instead, accountability loops should be light and real-time: weekly updates, milestone check-ins, and dashboards that provide visibility without slowing progress.

The goal is not control but confidence—confidence that decisions are moving quickly, lessons are being captured, and risks are being managed.

Do your oversight practices slow innovation, or do they enable it by providing disciplined trust?

5. Strong Mindset – Normalize Setbacks as Inputs for Growth

Boards must normalize setbacks. When a pilot fails, the right question is not "Who is at fault?" but "What did we learn, and how do we apply it?" Governance culture should reward adaptability.

This shift reframes failure as data. A missed milestone, a product that doesn't scale, or a market test that falls flat, each is a signal, not a scar. Boards that punish failure discourage experimentation. Boards that reframe failure as feedback encourage innovation and build long-term resilience.

In practice, this means celebrating lessons learned in board meetings, not hiding them. It means seeing disruption not as an exception, but as the default condition of business.

Does your board still measure success only in financial terms, or are you building a culture of adaptability? Do your executives fear failure, or do they see it as feedback?

Bringing It All Together

The **Agility Transfer Model** does not turn corporations into startups. Rather, it borrows the best of entrepreneurial practice—pilots, customer obsession, cash discipline, accountability, and grit-driven mindset—and adapts it to the scale and governance needs of legacy organizations.

For boards, the challenge is not to replace discipline with speed but to integrate them. Pilots with small bets create room for innovation. Expanding the definition of "customer" ensures relevance. Cash discipline sustains survival. Accountability loops balance speed and trust. And a strong mindset normalizes disruption as part of growth.

These principles are not theories. They are practical tools boards can apply immediately to shift culture and decision-making. The real question is whether your organization has the courage to move from perfection to iteration, from fear of failure to learning, and from rigid discipline to resilient adaptability.

Because in today's world, agility is not optional. It is the difference between governing transformation or governing decline.

A Global Lens on Agility

Agility looks different around the world. Having worked across five continents, I've seen how culture and context shape entrepreneurship.

In Africa, scarcity sparks ingenuity. Entrepreneurs repurpose materials, improvise logistics, and leverage community trust networks. Boards there learn that constraints can be accelerators.

In Latin America, family-run enterprises often combine agility with stewardship. Leaders move fast but remain accountable to communities and employees across generations. Boards learn that speed and responsibility are not opposites.

In Asia, scale comes quickly. Startups can grow from thousands to millions of users in months. But with scale comes scrutiny, which means governance must arrive earlier. Boards in Asia teach us that agility must be paired with structure sooner than in other regions.

For global companies, the lesson is clear: agility has universal value, but governance must adapt to local realities. *Does your governance framework assume one size fits all? Or are you adjusting to cultural context when you expand across borders?*

Lessons Executives Must Absorb

If you are a corporate director, agility is no longer a nice-to-have. It is survival. Disruption no longer gives you years to respond, it gives you months.

Executives must learn to:

- **Think in weeks, not years.** Planning cycles must match the speed of disruption.
- **Accept failure as learning, not shame.** Create a culture where pilots are rewarded even when they fail.
- **Value cash as much as profit.** Liquidity enables responsiveness when shocks come.
- **Embed agility into culture.** Make iteration part of daily life, not an occasional project.

In my governance work, I often tell boards: you don't need to be technologists or entrepreneurs. But you must absorb the lessons of entrepreneurial agility or risk becoming irrelevant.

Closing Reflection

Entrepreneurship is not exotic. It is the purest school of leadership. It teaches speed, accountability, and flexibility in ways no corporate training ever could.

Boards and executives who learn from entrepreneurship will not just survive disruption, they will govern transformation with confidence. Those who don't will find themselves governing decline.

Key Takeaway: Startups don't survive without agility. Now neither will corporations. Boards and executives must embrace disciplined speed, iterative learning, and adaptive endurance if they hope to lead the future.

Chapter 3

Resilience from Legacy Industries: Discipline and Adaptability in Action

The Core of Resilience

Every leader says they value resilience until they must prove it. During the COVID-19 pandemic, that test came suddenly and brutally. Overnight, supply chains collapsed, offices went dark, and teams scattered across living rooms and time zones. Companies that once thrived on long planning cycles were forced to make existential decisions in days. Leaders discovered that resilience isn't built in calm waters, it's built in crisis.

It's easy to speak of grit and adaptability when markets are stable, but the true test comes when uncertainty hits without warning: when a critical system fails, a revenue stream vanishes, or a crisis forces impossible choices. In those moments, you discover whether your organization was built for resilience or merely hoping for it. What happens when stability becomes the exception, not the rule? As a board member or executive, your answer to that question defines the legacy of your leadership.

Resilience is not forged in annual reports or strategy decks, it is built quietly, through systems, decisions, and habits that prepare organizations for the unexpected. It's the invisible muscle memory of governance, developed long before a crisis arrives. When tested, it determines whether your enterprise bends, breaks, or bounces back stronger.

Resilience is one of the most overused words in leadership conversations, but in practice, it is also one of the least understood. Too often, resilience is described as "bouncing back" after a crisis, as if leadership were simply about endurance. Yet resilience is more than endurance, it is the ability to adapt, transform, and sustain performance under pressure.

Legacy industries, whether industrials, manufacturing, energy, or consumer services, have long been laboratories for resilience. These industries operate across cycles of boom and bust, regulatory shifts, and constant safety risks. They show us that survival comes not from rigidity but from balancing discipline with adaptability.

In the energy industry and other industrial operations, resilience meant discipline: safety metrics, compliance systems, and long-cycle planning. In franchising, resilience meant adaptability: making daily decisions that instantly affected employees, franchisees, and customers. In startups, resilience meant speed: pivoting quickly under constant scarcity. Each environment sharpened a different dimension of resilience. Combined, they showed me that resilience is not a personal trait, it is a governance capability.

I learned these firsthand leading large-scale industrial operations, later as an entrepreneur running multi-site franchises, and more recently as an advisor and Board Member to startups. Each environment demanded resilience, but in different forms:

- **Discipline** in industrial operations where safety and compliance were non-negotiable.
- **Adaptability** in customer-facing businesses where daily fluctuations demanded instant decisions.
- **Speed** in startups where resource scarcity meant pivots were constant.

Together, these experiences taught me that resilience is not only something leaders simply possess, but also something organizations build, it's a leadership imperative for you and your organization. As a board member or executive, you can't delegate resilience, you must design it into your systems, your culture, and your strategy. It's not something you build after a crisis, it's what prepares you to face one. The lessons forged in legacy industries offer you a roadmap: discipline, flexibility, and foresight that can help your company, whether a startup or a multinational, endure disruption and emerge stronger. *So, are you building resilience by design, or only discovering it by accident when challenges arrive?*

Legacy industries might look slow from the outside, heavy with structure, regulation, and routine, but beneath that structure lies something invaluable: survival intelligence. Every safety rule, process map, and audit trail exists because someone, somewhere, learned a hard lesson about risk and consequence. These industries didn't become resilient by accident; they engineered resilience through discipline. And while startups often pride themselves on speed and flexibility, they can learn more from this endurance mindset than they realize. The secret is not to copy the bureaucracy but to extract the essence: how to combine adaptability with accountability, speed with structure, ambition with foresight.

As we move through this chapter, I want you to look at resilience not as theory, but as practice, lessons learned the hard way in industries that couldn't afford to fail. I've seen legacy sectors survive crises that would have broken younger companies, not because they were slow, but because they were disciplined. So, before you rush to dismiss the "old guard" as outdated, look again. The sectors that endure every cycle have mastered six enduring principles of resilience, principles that every modern organization, especially startups, must internalize if they want to scale without breaking. Together, we'll unpack what they can teach you and how you can apply them to make your organization stronger, faster, and ready for whatever comes next.

Lessons Startups Must Absorb from Legacy Industries

At first glance, legacy industries might look slow, bureaucratic, even outdated. But if you look closer, what you'll actually see is survival in motion. Every process, checklist, and safety review exists because someone learned the hard way what happens when it doesn't. These systems weren't built for control; they were built for endurance. Companies that have lasted decades or centuries didn't do so by chasing trends; they did it by mastering discipline, accountability, and foresight. If you're leading a startup, advising a board, or running an established enterprise, you can learn more from their playbook than you might think. Beneath the formality lies a simple truth: resilience is not a coincidence, it's a design.

So, ask yourself: *what lessons from those legacy organizations could make your own company stronger? Could you borrow their discipline without inheriting their bureaucracy? Could you apply their risk mindset without slowing down your innovation?* The principles are universal: discipline is the foundation of trust; accountability keeps you connected to every stakeholder; long-cycle thinking keeps you focused beyond the next quarter; redundancy protects you from shocks; reputation compounds like capital; and flexibility—the ability to scale up or down—determines who survives the downturn.

Discipline Is Non-Negotiable

In industrial sectors, discipline is not a bureaucratic burden, it is a survival tool. Compliance frameworks, safety processes, and quality controls exist not because leaders enjoy paperwork, but because lives and billions in capital are at stake.

I recall advising a global industrial manufacturer that faced growing vulnerabilities across its supply chain, shortages of critical materials, delays in key components, and an increasing scarcity of skilled labor. Volatility was no longer episodic; it had become systemic. Even small disruptions started to threaten costs, customer trust, and operational continuity.

What struck me wasn't the size of the problem but the discipline of their response. Instead of improvising, leadership treated risk management as a strategic capability. They mapped vulnerabilities across suppliers, prioritized risks by likelihood and impact, and built relationships that went beyond transactions. Diversification wasn't a spreadsheet exercise; it was a cultural one.

Over time, the results became visible. Delivery reliability improved, the frequency and severity of supply interruptions dropped, and customers noticed. Even when sector-wide disruptions hit, they kept operating. That experience reminded me how discipline, when embedded in governance, doesn't slow a company down, it anchors it when everything else starts to shake.

The board's insistence on discipline—not as red tape, but as strategic insurance—made the difference.

In your organization, do you see discipline as bureaucracy, or as the backbone of resilience? In times of disruption, would your systems hold under stress—or collapse because you treated discipline as optional?

Stakeholder Accountability

Resilience is not only about processes and systems. It is also about people, specifically, the many stakeholders who can make or break a company's survival. Legacy firms have long histories of managing investors, regulators, unions, employees, and communities. That balance is part of their resilience DNA.

Take the story of a multi-location service franchise. Rapid expansion doubled its footprint in under five years, but the speed created uneven customer experiences, cash-flow strain, and high staff turnover. Franchisees, the frontline stakeholders, felt neglected.

The board intervened. Leadership slowed expansion, consolidated operations, and introduced standardized processes. More importantly, they instituted verification loops. This built accountability across franchisees, employees, and managers.

The results spoke for themselves. Profitability improved, turnover fell by 20%, and customer satisfaction scores rose. Liquidity reserves gave the business the resilience to withstand a later downturn.

The lesson is simple: ignoring stakeholder accountability in pursuit of speed leads to fragility. Building trust, discipline, and verification into stakeholder relationships is what sustains resilience.

Have you mapped the hidden stakeholders in your ecosystem—beyond shareholders—who could define your resilience in crisis? Are you governing in a way that balances their competing expectations?

Long-Cycle Thinking

Resilient leaders zoom out. While startups often focus on growth sprints, legacy companies are used to modeling scenarios over decades. This long-cycle thinking may feel slow, but it provides an essential perspective when facing risks that can unfold over years or even decades.

Think of a large healthcare system preparing for public health emergencies. Long before a global pandemic arrived, its board required leadership to run scenario plans: *What if patient surges overwhelmed capacity? What if supply chains broke? What if funding collapsed?*

As part of those preparations, they invested in telehealth platforms, stockpiled critical supplies, and built relationships with multiple suppliers across regions. When crisis eventually struck, they were not improvising, they were executing.

The results: continuity of service, the ability to pivot staff across facilities, and the preservation of trust from patients and governments alike.

For boards, the takeaway is clear. Resilience is not about reacting to today's headlines; it is about preparing for shocks you can't yet imagine.

Are your strategies built only for the next quarter—or are you investing in resilience that will matter decades from now?

Redundancy and Safety Nets

Redundancy is often dismissed as inefficiency. But in truth, redundancy is resilience.

Consider the experience of a global consumer goods company. When geopolitical shocks disrupted raw material supplies, many competitors halted production. This company, however, had designed redundancy into its operations: diversified suppliers, alternate logistics routes, and reallocated production facilities.

At the time, some directors had questioned the cost of these "inefficiencies." But when disruption hit, they delivered 90% of orders while competitors failed. Customers rewarded reliability with loyalty, and the company gained market share.

Resilience in this case was not improvised in crisis, it was designed years earlier, embedded into governance.

In your organization, do you cut buffers in the name of efficiency, or do you recognize them as strategic insurance?

Reputation as an Asset

Resilience is not only measured in financial terms. Reputation, the trust you build with customers, employees, regulators, and society, is perhaps the most important currency of resilience.

Companies that invest in compliance, safety, and transparency early often survive crises better because stakeholders trust them to act responsibly. Conversely, those that dismiss reputation as "soft" find that trust evaporates quickly when tested.

I recall a consumer services enterprise that faced regulatory scrutiny after a crisis. What saved it was not only its operational response, but the reservoir of trust it had built over years: transparent communications, fair dealings with employees, and visible community engagement. Regulators gave it the benefit of the doubt, customers remained loyal, and employees stayed committed.

Founders and Boards must recognize that resilience is not only operational, it is reputational. And reputation, once lost, is nearly impossible to recover.

Is your board treating reputation as a line item on risk registers or as a core asset to be protected and invested in? Does your startup strategize how to build its reputation?

Resources to Scale Up (or Down)

Resilience is not only about endurance, but also about flexibility in motion. Too often, leaders equate resilience with expansion, assuming that strength means constant growth. But the ability to scale down can be just as vital as the ability to scale up. True resilience lies in flexing both ways, protecting the core when times are hard, and expanding decisively when opportunity returns.

Consider a regional enterprise that nearly collapsed when a global pandemic erased half its revenue in weeks. Instead of chasing new growth or taking on risky debt, the board acted swiftly. They paused non-essential projects, renegotiated supplier contracts, and preserved liquidity. Leadership communicated transparently explaining to employees and customers alike that protecting cash flow was not retreat, but resilience. Six months later, those reserves became their lifeline. When competitors folded, the company used its preserved capital to acquire distressed assets and expand market share. Their survival wasn't luck, it was design. The board had treated liquidity as a strategic asset, not an afterthought.

A similar lesson came from a global engineering company that builds components for aircraft, renewable systems, and advanced manufacturing. For years, efficiency was their mantra: centralized plants, long production runs, and finely tuned supply chains. It all worked until it didn't. As electrification surged and energy prices spiked, the same model that once ensured stability became a liability. The company found itself optimized for predictability in a world that had become unpredictable. Sound familiar? Many leaders find themselves in that same trap, an organization built for growth but unable to contract without breaking.

To survive, the company reframed flexibility as a governance principle. Instead of building another mega-factory, they invested in modular production hubs that could scale with demand. They maintained liquidity buffers, diversified suppliers, and introduced "governance triggers", predefined conditions that guided when to accelerate or pause investment. During board reviews, in addition to ask, *"How much did we grow?"* they started asking, *"How quickly could we pivot if the market turned tomorrow?"*

When a regulatory shift later reduced demand in one region, they didn't scramble. Production was reallocated within weeks, customers remained served, and financial stability held. Six months later, when demand rebounded, they scaled up again, smoothly, without chaos or layoffs. What used to be reaction became capability. That's what resource flexibility looks like: turning volatility into advantage.

The lesson for you as a leader is clear, your organization's strength doesn't come from size alone. It comes from design. Liquidity, partnerships, and modular capabilities are not inefficiencies; they are insurance against fragility. In fact, resilience increasingly depends on your strategic partnerships, alliances with suppliers, distributors, and even competitors that can share capacity, data, and logistics when markets shift. The companies that treat partnerships as extensions of their ecosystem, not transactions, gain flexibility far beyond their balance sheet.

Do your systems allow you to flex both ways or are you only built for growth in good times? If demand dropped 30% tomorrow, could your organization downshift with discipline rather than panic?

Framework – The Resilience Transfer Model

So how can startups, boards, and executives embed resilience without suffocating agility? The danger is real: lean too heavily on efficiency and you create brittleness; lean too heavily on speed and you invite fragility. The solution lies in balance. I call this the **Resilience Transfer Model**, six practices drawn from legacy industries but adapted for today's disrupted environment, Safety and Discipline as Strategic Priorities, Stakeholder Mapping, Scenario Planning, Redundancy by Design, Reputation as an Asset and Resources to Scale Up (or Down). These practices are as relevant to a founder running a 10-person startup as they are to directors sitting on a century-old corporation's board.

If you are a startup founder, these practices can feel counterintuitive as you're trained to move fast, improvise, and stretch every dollar. If you are a corporate director, these practices may feel obvious but underused as your systems have discipline, but agility often dies in process. Either way, resilience is not built by accident. It is designed

1. Safety and Discipline as Strategic Priorities

In legacy industries, safety is never negotiable. One misstep in an aircraft operation, a refinery, or a chemical plant can cost lives, billions of dollars, and reputational collapse. That is why these companies treat discipline as equal to financial performance.

Startups often dismiss safety and compliance as "big company problems." But governance should never accept shortcuts. Safety and compliance do not slow growth, they enable it by providing trust and predictability.

For boards, this means embedding safety metrics into dashboards, elevating compliance discussions to the boardroom, and treating near-misses as learning opportunities rather than nuisances. For founders, it means building the mindset early: a product that breaks customer trust, even once, may never get a second chance.

Are your executives under pressure to move fast without safety nets? Does your governance system elevate discipline to the same level as growth targets?

2. Stakeholder Mapping

Legacy firms have long navigated webs of stakeholders—investors, regulators, unions, employees, governments, and communities. They know resilience depends on balancing often competing expectations.

Startups, by contrast, often see only one stakeholder: the end user. But resilience demands a broader map. In franchising, for example, franchisees are as critical as consumers. In biotech, regulators may be the make-or-break "customer." In SaaS, investors and distribution partners can determine survival as much as end users do.

Boards and founders should identify stakeholders early, map their interests, and anticipate conflicts before they erupt. Mechanisms such as stakeholder councils, transparent reporting, and regular engagement with employees or community groups reduce blind spots and build credibility.

Have you defined your true stakeholders—or are you still listening only to shareholders and quarterly earnings? As a founder, have you truly identified your stakeholders?

3. Scenario Planning

Legacy industries are built to think in decades. They model oil cycles, infrastructure projects, or regulatory shifts that may take generations to unfold. This long-cycle thinking is one of their greatest resilience strengths.

For startups and corporates alike, scenario planning does not mean predicting the future. It means rehearsing plausible futures and testing how the organization would respond. *What if your supply chain is cut off tomorrow? What if your flagship technology is leapfrogged? What if a funding round falls through?*

Boards should demand scenario planning annually not as an academic workshop but as a strategic rehearsal. For founders, the discipline of asking "*What if?*" can mean the difference between collapse and reinvention.

Is your organization planning only for growth or are you rehearsing survival and reinvention? As a startup founder, have you identified the entire market potential and run the what ifs?

4. Redundancy by Design

Efficiency is celebrated in modern business culture. But too much efficiency creates brittleness. Legacy firms understand redundancy, multiple suppliers, backup systems, and liquidity reserves as insurance rather than waste.

In today's interconnected world, a single weak link can shut down operations. Startups that run razor-thin operations often crumble when a supplier falters or a system outage strikes. Even lightweight redundancies like cross-training employees, diversifying vendors, or keeping a modest cash buffer, can mean survival.

Boards should treat buffers not as inefficiency, but as strategic assets. Startups should see redundancy not as a luxury, but as an early discipline.

Are your executives rewarded for short-term efficiency at the expense of long-term resilience?

5. Reputation as an Asset

Resilience is not only operational; it is reputational. Companies with deep reservoirs of trust survive crises better than those with shaky credibility. Regulators give them leeway. Customers give them the benefit of the doubt. Employees stay loyal in tough times.

Boards must elevate reputation to a governance priority. That means embedding ethics, transparency, and compliance into culture not as "soft" initiatives, but as central assets. For founders, it means realizing that a single misstep, whether a data breach, labor dispute, or misleading claim, can derail growth or scare off investors.

Protecting reputation means more than PR, it means transparent crisis communication, ethical sourcing, visible community investment, and values that guide tough decisions.

Does your leadership treat reputation as a strategic asset, or as an afterthought to earnings calls and pitch decks? Do you have a strategic approach for your startup reputation?

6. Resources to Scale Up (or Down)

Growth is seductive. Startups often see scaling as the only direction worth planning for, while corporates too often assume size itself guarantees resilience. But true resilience requires the ability to scale both ways, expanding quickly when opportunities emerge and contracting responsibly when downturns hit.

Legacy industries have mastered this rhythm. They expand capacity during booms and contract during recessions without dismantling their core. By contrast, startups that grow recklessly often burn through cash and collapse when external shocks demand contraction. The lesson is simple: scaling down is not failure, it is survival strategy.

Boards and founders must embed flexibility into their resource models. This includes workforce arrangements that can flex without eroding morale, liquidity buffers that allow breathing room, and asset-light strategies that make pivots feasible. Overcommitting to fixed costs, long-term leases, bloated headcounts, or rigid supplier contracts, erodes adaptability and magnifies fragility.

Equally important is the role of strategic partnerships. Partnerships with suppliers, distributors, or technology allies can expand capacity without heavy capital commitments, while joint ventures or alliances can share risks during downturns. For startups, partnerships provide credibility and scale they cannot build alone. For corporates, they inject agility and innovation without overextending resources.

Resilience in scaling is not about chasing constant growth, it is about managing cycles with foresight, creativity, and discipline.

Are your partnerships built for shared growth or shared resilience? And most importantly, do your board's signal when to slow down as confidently as they do when to grow?

Bringing It All Together

The **Resilience Transfer Model** does not turn corporations into startups, or startups into corporations. Instead, it borrows the best of legacy resilience practices—safety, stakeholder mapping, scenario planning, redundancy, reputation, and flexible resources—and adapts them for both worlds.

For boards, the challenge is not to replace discipline with speed, but to integrate them. For founders, the challenge is not to abandon agility, but to embed discipline into it.

These are not theories. They are tools you can apply immediately. Whether your organization is a 100-year-old enterprise or a 10-person startup, the real question is: does it have the courage to shift from rigid efficiency to resilient adaptability, from measuring success only in quarterly returns to designing systems that can survive decades of disruption?

Because in today's world, resilience is not optional. It is the difference between governing transformation or governing decline.

Global Lens on Resilience

Resilience may be universal in principle, but it looks different depending on where you stand in the world. Across regions, cultures, and industries, organizations express resilience through different instincts, some through collective adaptability, others through long-term stewardship or resource discipline. Understanding these nuances helps you, as a leader or board member, shape resilience that fits your context rather than importing it blindly from another.

In **Africa**, resilience often means creativity under constraint. Leaders build systems that work despite limitations, where supply chains are uncertain, infrastructure unreliable, and capital limited. Yet innovation flourishes because people are trained to adapt from day one. Ask yourself: *could your organization operate with half its resources and still deliver impact? If not, you have efficiency but not yet resilience.*

In **Asia**, resilience takes shape through discipline and foresight. Many firms plan across decades, embedding scenario thinking and quality assurance deep into their cultures. Leaders emphasize collective accountability, resilience as a shared duty, not an individual act of heroism. This mindset is what allows them to rebound from shocks with coordination rather than chaos. So, *have you built systems that enable people to respond consistently, or are you still relying on a few heroes in every crisis?*

In **Europe**, resilience has become synonymous with responsibility. Companies navigate tight regulations, energy transitions, and societal expectations that force long-term balance between profit and sustainability. Their resilience is institutional, rooted in governance frameworks, risk registers, and ethical oversight. The takeaway is clear: resilience isn't reactive; it's designed through governance. *How well does your governance structure anticipate, not just respond to, disruption?*

And in the **United States**, resilience often shows up as reinvention. The willingness to pivot, to rebuild, to fail publicly and try again, is a cultural advantage. Yet the same culture of speed can erode discipline if not anchored in governance. *How many of your boardroom conversations celebrate reinvention and how many truly sustain it?*

Across continents, one truth holds: resilience is contextual, but its essence is universal: discipline plus adaptability, purpose plus flexibility. Whether you lead in São Paulo, Singapore, Stockholm, or Houston, resilience must live not just in your crisis playbooks, but in your daily governance.

Does your organization's model of resilience fit its cultural and economic context? Have you learned from how others across the globe survive disruption differently?

Because in the age of interconnected crises, resilience built in isolation is fragility disguised. The strongest organizations don't just recover, they learn from every geography, every industry, every shock, and use that learning to build forward stronger than before.

From my perspective, executives, founders and boards must:

- Balance agility with discipline.
- Treat cash as a strategic resource.
- Protect reputation as a non-negotiable asset.
- Build systems and strategic partnerships that can scale both up and down.
- Design resilience into governance, not bolt it on in crisis.

So, in your organization or board, is resilience part of your governance culture or just a crisis plan in a binder?

Closing Reflection

Resilience is not about bouncing back, it is about designing organizations that can absorb shocks, adapt quickly, and sustain trust. It is about building forward. It is not what you do after disruption; it is how you prepare for it before it arrives. The strongest organizations do not wait for storms to test their strength; they anticipate the winds and reinforce their foundations. Legacy industries remind us that discipline and adaptability are not opposites but complements.

For you as a leader, the challenge is to make resilience visible and intentional, embedded in how your teams plan, how your systems flex, and how your culture responds under pressure. Whether you lead a startup striving to scale or a global enterprise navigating constant volatility, resilience is your ultimate competitive advantage. Startups that ignore discipline risk fragility; corporations that ignore agility risk irrelevance. The future belongs to boards and executives who can combine both.

Ask yourself: *if tomorrow brought another shock, a market crash, a supply breakdown, or a technology failure, would your organization bend and recover, or would it fracture under the weight of surprise? What habits of governance, what investments in people, what reserves of trust are you building today to withstand that test?*

Because in the end, resilience is not endurance, it is evolution. It is the capacity to adapt without losing purpose, to transform without losing integrity, and to emerge from every disruption not just intact, but improved. It is disciplined adaptability with resources ready to flex in either direction.

Resilience is not a reaction; it is a design choice. Resilience isn't measured by how high you climb, it's measured by how well you can bend, rebalance, and rise again when the world changes direction. Leaders who embed it intentionally will not just survive disruption; they will define the next era of stability and growth. Those who don't will find themselves governing decline.

Chapter 4

The Board and AI Oversight: Balancing Innovation and Accountability

In one boardroom, the mahogany table gleamed under recessed lights as directors reviewed a 200-slide deck filled with metrics, forecasts, and compliance charts. It was a global enterprise, proud of its systems and legacy. The CEO spoke confidently about "digital transformation" and "operational efficiency." When the topic of artificial intelligence appeared midway through the agenda, a director asked, "Do we have an AI strategy?" The CIO nodded. "Yes, we're exploring machine learning pilots." The conversation moved on. Ten minutes later, the meeting returned to quarterly margins.

Across town, three founders met around a coffee-stained table in a co-working space. Their "board" consisted of a single investor and a whiteboard crowded with scribbles. They debated whether to integrate an open-source AI model into their product. "It could triple engagement," one argued. "Or tank our trust if it goes wrong," said another. They didn't call it "AI governance," but that's exactly what it was, a decision about risk, ethics, and accountability.

Two boardrooms, two worlds. Yet both were asking the same question: How do we lead when algorithms start making decisions we can't fully explain?

The truth is that artificial intelligence has blurred the line between technology and governance. It is no longer a "topic" on the agenda; it is the agenda shaping strategy, influencing behavior, and redefining the board's duty of care. AI oversight is not technical; it is a governance duty rooted in accountability and trust.

Both rooms, though worlds apart, were confronting the same quiet revolution, one not of technology, but of accountability

This chapter will help you understand what effective AI oversight really looks like from the boardroom. You'll learn how leading organizations are integrating AI into strategy, balancing innovation with accountability, and asking the right questions to build trust and resilience.

So, as you read this chapter, ask yourself: *Does your board treat AI as a strategic priority with time, debate and dissent or as an occasional update from the CIO? Do your governance systems balance innovation with accountability or rely on luck to stay compliant?*

The New Governance Reality: When Technology Outruns Oversight

Artificial intelligence is changing boardrooms faster than most directors realize. In many organizations, AI oversight today resembles cybersecurity oversight fifteen years ago: fragmented updates, limited fluency at the board level, and a quiet assumption that "the tech people" have it handled. That is not bad intent; it is a sign of a new responsibility outpacing old habits.

Ten years ago, AI was an experiment. Today, it quietly runs credit approvals, job screenings, safety alerts, maintenance schedules, and customer service conversations. The systems are invisible, but their decisions carry moral, legal, and reputational weight.

In many boards, the conversation remains stuck at the surface: "How much are we investing in AI?" or "Will automation replace people?" But the real questions cut deeper: How do we know the data is unbiased? Who takes responsibility when an algorithm fails? What happens if customers lose trust?

In a logistics board meeting, a director celebrated their new AI routing engine until community complaints flooded in. Their predictive routing tool promised to optimize fuel usage and delivery times. It worked until it began over-prioritizing urban routes and under-serving rural areas. The algorithm hadn't been designed to consider equity of service, and soon, community backlash turned a success story into a reputational crisis. The board realized too late that governance had to include not just results, but how those results were achieved.

AI didn't just optimize routes; it exposed blind spots in what the company considered fairness

Does your board treat AI as a line item or as a strategic capability? When you hear "automation," do you also hear "accountability"? If an AI system made a contested decision yesterday, denied a loan, rejected a résumé, flagged a safety incident, would your board even know? Would you know who owns accountability when that decision is challenged?

The Governance Blind Spot: AI as the Next Sarbanes–Oxley Moment

AI oversight is where cybersecurity was fifteen years ago which every board agrees it matters, but few have real accountability. Too often, AI appears as a line item in "technology updates," delegated to CIOs or data scientists, rarely discussed by the full board.

During a governance review with a large financial services firm, one director told me candidly, "We rely on management to tell us if the AI is working." It was an honest admission but a dangerous one. The board had impressive financial oversight, yet no one could explain who was accountable for algorithmic outcomes. As one executive later reflected, "We treated the models like black boxes that only our data scientists understood." Governance cannot be outsourced to engineers or buried in dashboards. The board's duty isn't to write code, it's to ensure accountability: who owns the outcomes, who monitors the risks, and what happens when systems fail.

I remember a recent case which a global consumer goods company learned this the hard way. Its AI-powered pricing engine delivered record margins until reporters revealed that low-income neighborhoods were paying higher prices. The model had optimized profit, not fairness. Regulators intervened, customers rebelled, and the board was blindsided. The failure wasn't in technology; it was in governance.

Every director remembers how Sarbanes–Oxley redefined corporate accountability. AI is today's equivalent: the next great test of fiduciary duty. But this time, the challenge isn't compliance, it's comprehension. You can't govern what you don't understand.

Progressive boards are responding by building AI literacy. They host teach-ins, bring in external experts, and even simulate AI failures. One financial institution held a live demo showing how a single data change, like an employment gap, altered loan outcomes. It didn't make the directors data scientists, but it made them sharper, more curious, and better at asking the right questions.

Can your board explain, in one sentence, how AI is used in your organization and who is accountable for it? Would you know if it failed? Could you defend your oversight to a regulator tomorrow?

AI oversight belongs in governance, where accountability and trust, not technical mastery, are the core concerns.

Building the Framework: From Policy to Practice

AI governance is not about bureaucracy; it's about designing confidence systems, structures that ensure AI aligns with strategy, ethics, and law. A mature framework typically rests on four pillars: oversight, accountability, transparency, and adaptability.

Oversight means clearly assigning who reports on AI and how often. Whether through a technology committee or the full board, someone must own the conversation.

Accountability means mapping decision rights: who approves AI use cases, who signs off risk levels, who reports breaches.

Transparency demands explainability. Directors must insist that key systems can be described in plain language. If your management team can't explain how a model decides, that's a red flag.

Adaptability ensures proportionality. Oversight should match the level of risk. A chatbot doesn't require the same scrutiny as an AI medical device or credit-scoring engine.

One global bank now uses a "tiered AI review" system. High-impact models, those influencing credit, hiring, or compliance, require full board disclosure. Lower-risk applications, like marketing personalization, follow lighter, internal reviews. The policy is simple but powerful: scrutiny scales with consequence.

You can think of it as air traffic control for innovation. Every plane (AI system) has clearance levels, checklists, and communication protocols. Some fly close to the ground; others carry passengers through storms. The governance role is not to ground the fleet, it's to make sure none crash into each other.

Does your organization know which AI systems pose high risk? Are you proportioning oversight to impact, or treating all AI the same? Do your governance documents, committee charters, reporting lines, escalation paths, reflect this new reality? If your board adopted a tiered AI review tomorrow, which systems would qualify for top-tier scrutiny and who would decide?

Alignment with Strategy, Goals, Values, and Ethics

Corporate governance ensures that what a company builds reflects what it stands for. AI is no exception. True oversight begins not with technical specifications but with strategic intent: *What problem are we solving, and how does this system advance our goals without compromising our values and aligning to our company strategy?*

AI cannot sit in a silo, not in your organization. It must live at the center of strategy, shaping how you compete, how you serve customers, and how your teams learn. If your board treats AI as an isolated "innovation project," you risk chasing efficiency while losing sight of purpose. But when your board integrates AI into the corporate compass, strategy, ethics, and culture, the technology becomes an enabler of your mission, not a distraction from it.

I once worked with a health network that used AI to optimize appointment scheduling. The first model was efficient, it maximized throughput. But the board asked a different question: "What outcome defines success for us, volume or continuity of care?" The second version of the tool prioritized long-term relationships, scheduling patients with familiar doctors and offering flexible windows to reduce no-shows. The difference wasn't technical, it was philosophical. The algorithm began serving the mission, not just the metric.

A global retailer faced a similar dilemma with dynamic pricing. During emergencies, its algorithm spiked prices according to demand. Technically, it worked perfectly. Ethically, it failed. The board intervened, adding fairness constraints and "event caps." Short-term profits fell, but reputation—and customer loyalty—rose.

In both cases, the technology stayed the same and what changed was the question the board chose to ask.

As a director or executive, your duty is to ensure that objective reflects your strategy and ethics. *When your board approves AI spending, are you endorsing a technology or a purpose-driven outcome? If your algorithm could answer the question "What does winning look like?", would its definition match your organization's values? And most importantly, is AI embedded in your enterprise strategy or orbiting outside it, unaligned and unexamined?*

AI doesn't just execute strategy, it shapes it. The question is whether it's shaping yours by design or by default.

When Governance Meets Culture: The Human Side of AI

Technology is easy compared to people. The hardest part of AI oversight is not technical literacy but cultural readiness.

I once observed two companies introduce nearly identical AI systems, one succeeded, one failed. The difference? Culture. The first company encouraged "algorithmic humility": employees could challenge system outputs without fear. The second treated the AI as infallible. Within months, resentment grew, frontline workers quietly ignored recommendations, and performance suffered.

Boards play a crucial role in setting tone. If leadership glorifies AI as magic, employees will defer uncritically. If leadership treats AI as a tool, powerful but fallible, then curiosity and responsibility coexist.

A manufacturing company's safety team once stopped a line because its AI sensor flagged a potential hazard. Later, the alert turned out to be a false positive. The board didn't punish the stoppage; instead, it applauded the vigilance. "Better a false alarm than a missed warning," the chair said. That single comment set a cultural precedent: use AI, but question it.

AI oversight begins in code but matures in culture. Without psychological safety, transparency dies. Without transparency, trust erodes. And without trust, no technology, no matter how advanced, can sustain performance.

Does your culture allow people to question AI outcomes openly? How do you reward curiosity and caution? Do your employees know when to escalate concerns and that they'll be heard when they do?

Accountable AI: Turning Principles into Practice

The term "Responsible AI" sounds good and relevant. "Accountable AI" is harder, it demands proof.

True accountability means AI decisions can be traced, explained, and corrected. It means knowing who is responsible, to whom, and for what. Boards should view Accountable AI not as a policy checkbox but as a governance architecture connecting ethics to operations.

Here's what that looks like in practice:

1. **Clear Ownership** – Define which executive owns AI oversight (CIO, CDO, or Chief Ethics Officer). Accountability must flow up to the board, not sideways across departments.
2. **Explainability** – Require plain-language documentation of key models. If a director cannot understand how a decision was made, it cannot be approved.

3. **Auditability** – Ensure independent validation, internal audit or third-party review, of algorithms with material impact.
4. **Human Oversight** – Keep a human in the loop for high-stakes applications like safety, finance, or healthcare.
5. **Stakeholder Responsibility** – Extend accountability beyond shareholders to customers, regulators, employees, and communities.
6. **Specific Metrics** – Implement clear metrics AI solutions selection, implementation, performance and ROI

A few years ago, a technology firm made headlines as they learned this in the hard way. Its HR algorithm screened job applications automatically. It was efficient until an internal whistleblower revealed that the model was amplifying gender bias. The board launched an independent audit, published the findings, and established a new policy: every AI model affecting people's lives must have a named human owner.

By naming every model's human owner, they made accountability visible again and trust returned and eventually attracted new talent who saw the company as a leader in ethical innovation. Accountability wasn't a cost; it became a differentiator.

If an AI system in your organization caused harm tomorrow, could you trace responsibility? Does your audit committee review algorithmic risks, or only financial ones? Are your governance structures clear enough for accountability to survive leadership transitions? Are your metrics clear and sufficient to estimate and measure the investment ROI?

Innovation Without Bureaucracy: Small Bets, Clear Checkpoints

Governance is not a break. It is a steering wheel. To keep speed and safety together, boards can encourage small bets with clear gate criteria:

- **Pilots** with explicit success metrics (value, fairness, satisfaction) and kill criteria if thresholds aren't met.
- **Sandboxes** to test with synthetic or limited data first.
- **Canary releases** to a tiny cohort before broad launch.
- **Customer councils** or **employee advisory panels** to surface qualitative feedback early.
- **Budget guardrails** that release more funding only when defined, measurable learning has occurred.

One payments startup I followed closely scaled globally by shipping weekly and auditing monthly. The board implemented a discipline I admired: no new market launch without a fairness review, and no partner integration without a rollback plan. That cadence—fast moves, hard checks—kept innovation alive and reputational debt low.

Where in your organization does innovation die under "big bet" theater, and where could small, instrumented bets move you faster with less risk?

Vendor and Model Dependence: Don't Outsource Accountability

Third-party models and APIs are powerful and risky. The convenience of "plug-and-play" can become a single point of failure or a reputational conduit you do not control. Boards should ask for a dependency map: critical vendors, data processors, model providers, their compliance posture, and where you have exit options.

One enterprise learned this when a generative provider changed terms, throttling access during peak season. Because the company had already built a dual-source strategy and limited hard coupling to one vendor's idiosyncrasies, operations continued with minimal disruption.

If your top model provider turned off access tomorrow, what would break and what have you already done to make sure "everything" is not the answer?

Global Context: Governance Without Borders

Artificial intelligence doesn't stop at national boundaries, and neither should governance. The challenge for global boards is that AI ethics, regulation, and social expectations vary dramatically. When I worked with teams across Europe and Asia, I saw firsthand how one word 'trust' meant different things in each culture.

Europe treats AI through the lens of rights, transparency, human dignity, data protection. The European Union's AI Act assigns responsibility based on risk level and emphasizes explainability. In the United States, the approach is fragmented, innovation first, regulation second. In Asia, scale and efficiency dominate; oversight often follows deployment rather than preceding it.

For multinationals, this creates a governance puzzle. A company might deploy one model globally but face five different regulatory expectations. An industrial manufacturer, for instance, discovered that its predictive maintenance tool, trained in the U.S., violated emerging data transfer rules in Europe. The board's solution wasn't a legal workaround, but a governance redesign: a regional AI oversight committee empowered to adapt policies locally while reporting globally.

The result was not uniformity but resilience. Each market operated within a common ethical compass, yet with autonomy to adapt. That balance between central principle and local nuance is what defines modern AI governance.

Does your AI policy travel well across borders, or does it assume one-size-fits-all? Have you defined what "responsible AI" means in your cultural context? If your company operated in a country with stricter or looser AI norms, would your governance still hold?

From Risk to Resilience: The Board's Role Ahead

The question for tomorrow's boardroom is no longer "Should we use AI?" it's "Are we governing it wisely?" That single distinction will determine whether AI becomes a multiplier of innovation or a source of existential risk.

One multinational company learned this lesson through crisis. Its customer service chatbot, designed to reduce call center costs, began spreading misinformation after a data update. Within hours, screenshots went viral, customers lost trust, and the CEO issued a public apology. During the board's post-mortem, one director reflected quietly: "We treated AI as a technology problem. It was a governance problem."

That realization changed everything. The board created an AI Ethics Charter, added quarterly model reviews to its risk dashboard, and launched companywide AI literacy workshops. Within a year, employee confidence and customer trust had risen higher than before the incident. That is what governance maturity looks like moving from panic to preparedness, from reaction to resilience.

Resilient boards don't just respond to crises; they design systems that prevent them. The shift starts with structure clear expectations and simple rules that translate principles into practice.

Boards that lead in AI oversight do five things well: they align every model to strategy and ethics; tier risk proportionally; define clear human oversight; maintain concise, living policies; and establish feedback loops that learn faster than failure.

When boards embed these disciplines, AI oversight stops being a compliance checklist and becomes a resilience system, one that can anticipate shocks, contain failures, and recover stronger.

The throughline is simple: AI oversight is not technical; it is a governance duty rooted in accountability and trust.

Does your board have an AI readiness plan that's as robust as your cybersecurity framework? When you hear the term machine learning, do you think of opportunity or liability? Are you building a governance system that reacts to errors or one that prevents them? If tomorrow's headlines named your company in an AI-related incident, could you confidently explain your safeguards to investors, regulators, and the public?

The next era of governance will not be measured by how fast companies adopt AI, but by how wisely they steward it. The boards that recognize this now—embedding oversight into strategy, culture, and accountability—will not only protect their organizations; they will define the new standard for leadership in the age of intelligent machines.

Closing Reflection: Governing the Invisible

The most consequential technologies in your company will not arrive with warning labels. They will emerge quietly in dashboards, in workflows, in the subtle logic of how decisions are made. A pricing model adjusts automatically. A recruiting algorithm filters candidates before a human ever reviews them. A safety alert flashes not because a person raised concern, but because the machine did. And in that quiet shift, power changes hands from people to patterns.

That is why governance matters. Its purpose is to make the invisible visible, to surface what has been automated, and to ensure that every system, no matter how intelligent, still answers to human judgment, strategic intent, and ethical clarity.

As a director or executive, you may never write a line of code, but you bear a far greater responsibility: to ask the questions that enthusiasm avoids, to demand transparency where metrics obscure meaning, and to protect dignity and trust even when efficiency tempts you to look away. AI does not eliminate the need for governance, it multiplies it. The faster decisions move, the more essential oversight becomes.

When the next test arrives — and it will — your stakeholders will not measure your success by how advanced your algorithms were, but by how principled your leadership proved to be. *Did you use AI to act with speed and integrity, or did you let automation decide in your name?*

In the end, governance is not a barrier to innovation; it is the architecture of trust that lets organizations run fast without running blind. In tomorrow's boardrooms, that trust will be your greatest technology.

Chapter 5

Governance for Startups vs. Large Corporations and Non-Profit Organizations

Right-Sized Governance Enables Startups to Scale and Corporates to Innovate Without Losing Control

Governance as Context

Every boardroom tells a story, of speed, of structure, of how power and responsibility collide. Walk into three boardrooms in the same month and you'll feel three different climates. In one, a five-person startup is deciding whether to delay payroll so they can pay a cloud bill. In another, a public company's audit committee is grilling management on the footnotes to a footnote. In a third, a non-profit board is debating whether to expand a program that has community support but uncertain funding. Each room has the same word painted on the door—board—but what happens inside is governed by context.

I've served across this spectrum, global corporates, entrepreneurial ventures, and non-profits, and the pattern is unmistakable: governance must be right-sized. Too much structure too early can suffocate innovation. Too little discipline at scale can destroy everything you've built. The art of leadership is not choosing between control and creativity but knowing when to flex toward each.

Is your board creating clarity and velocity, or complexity and drag? If you removed half your governance tomorrow, what would break? If you doubled it, what would stall? is your governance designed to enable your organization's next stage of growth, or is it trapping you in its last?

As you read this chapter, you'll see how governance is not a one-size-fits-all template but a living system that adapts to scale, speed, and purpose. Whether you lead a startup fighting for runway or a corporation defending market share, this chapter will show how right-sized governance unlocks both agility and accountability helping you build organizations that move fast without breaking trust.

The Startup Board: Where Every Decision Feels Existential

When you step into a startup boardroom, the air feels different. There are no polished decks with months of preparation, no 50-page committee reports, and often no buffer of time between decision and consequence. Instead, there's urgency, raw ambition, and a sense that every choice, funding round, key hire, product pivot, could determine survival.

Startups live and die by speed, funding, and adaptability. Governance here isn't about compliance calendars or quarterly cycles; it's about ensuring survival today while keeping an eye on tomorrow. Unlike large corporations where processes are designed to slow down reckless behavior, startups operate in environments which moving too slowly can be fatal. For board members, this means your role isn't to police, but to empower without sacrificing accountability.

The boardroom of a startup is as much a coaching table as it is a governance body. Directors must bring a toolkit that balances agility with guidance:

- **Entrepreneurial Agility** – Markets shift weekly, sometimes daily. A director who cannot live with ambiguity will struggle. Agility isn't just desirable, it's survival.

- **Fundraising Acumen** – Directors are often rainmakers, connecting founders to capital.

- **Go-to-Market Expertise** – Strategy here isn't theoretical. Helping a founder refine pricing, test distribution channels, or negotiate the first enterprise customer can make the difference between traction and irrelevance.

- **Talent Building** – The right introductions for a CFO or technical lead can redefine the company's trajectory.

- **Hands-On Mentorship** – A startup board member must be willing to roll up their sleeves reviewing pitch decks, testing product demos, or making intros directly.

If you were sitting on a startup board today, could you bring this kind of immediate, tactical value or would you default to the long-cycle habits of corporate oversight?

Startup boards also operate on alignment, not formality. Many directors take equity instead of cash, signaling shared fate. Meetings are conversations, not rituals. The language is informal, yet the stakes are absolute: survival or failure. Instead of committee reports, you're more likely to hear frank questions: How many weeks of cash are left? Which customers are on the fence? What must we do before the next funding round?

For many corporate directors, this can be a shock. But it is also liberating: startup boards strip governance to its essentials.

If domestic startups are chaotic, global startups are chaos squared. When the startup crosses borders, the complexity multiplies: GDPR meets U.S. privacy rules; fundraising terms change across currencies; hiring culture shifts with time zones. I once watched a founder in São Paulo navigate investor expectations from Silicon Valley and data compliance from Brussels all before his Series B closed. The board's role was to add perspective, not pressure minimizing panic and not progress.

For board members, global awareness becomes as important as fundraising or product advice. The challenge is not only navigating regulations but also translating governance across cultures. *Would your current governance frameworks survive if stretched across three continents? Or would they collapse under the weight of complexity?*

Why Every Decision Feels Existential

In startups, the stakes are compressed. One misstep, a failed launch, a key hire leaving, a misjudged regulatory issue can shorten runway from months to weeks. Boards must balance speed with foresight: ensuring that survival decisions today don't compromise credibility tomorrow.

I've sat in rooms where founders debated cutting half their staff to extend runway. In those moments, the board isn't just a legal overseer, it's a sounding board, a coach, and sometimes a moral compass. Survival matters, but so does the way survival is achieved.

As a corporate director, you don't want to mimic startup chaos, but you do want to absorb its urgency. Ask yourself: *Does your board treat time as infinite? Do your executives believe they have months or years to adapt to disruption? Because in today's world, even corporates face startup-like pressures.*

The Public Company Board: The Pinnacle of Scrutiny

Public company boards live on a glass stage. Every move is visible to regulators, investors, proxy advisors, activists, and increasingly, to society at large. Unlike startups that can pivot quietly, or private companies that make decisions in the shadows, public companies must defend every choice in real time under relentless visibility. The danger is to become prisoners of compliance and quarterly guidance, where survival becomes about "checking the box." The discipline is to meet those obligations and still leave oxygen for strategy and innovation.

Key Skills in Public Boards

- **Regulatory Mastery:** Sarbanes–Oxley, disclosure rules, insider trading controls—these are non-negotiable. Directors cannot delegate literacy in these areas.

- **Risk Oversight:** Boards must see around corners, engaging proactively on cybersecurity, AI governance, climate risk, and geopolitical shocks. In public companies, the unasked question often becomes the biggest liability.

- **Capital Market Fluency:** Analysts, proxy advisors, and institutional investors shape the degrees of freedom management has. Directors must understand capital markets not as background noise, but as active forces shaping corporate destiny.

- **Committee Expertise:** Audit, Compensation, and Governance committees each require deep specialization. The audit chair must know the rulebook, the compensation chair must hold the line on pay-for-performance, and the governance chair must guide succession and culture.

- **Strategic Stewardship:** The heart of public company governance is balance—quarterly pressures versus long-term resilience.

Processes are formal, reporting is exhaustive, and liability is real. Compensation is structured with cash retainers and equity, and the workload is heavy. Missteps are not abstract, they spark lawsuits, reputational crises, and in some cases, board turnover.

I once watched a public board facing down an activist campaign. Their defense wasn't a poison pill, but transparent engagement. They sharpened their capital allocation story, invited dialogue with investors, and treated the activist not as a villain to fight but as a signal to refine their strategy. In the end, governance became a dialogue rather than a defense mechanism. That episode underscored a key truth: resilience in public company governance comes from engagement, not entrenchment.

When the company is multinational, risk compounds: sanctions, ESG supply-chain disclosures, cultural expectations colliding. One consumer brand faced backlash after a supplier failed labor standards overseas. The board didn't issue a defensive statement; they built a supplier-governance system with audits, remediation, public updates. Trust wasn't repaired overnight, but it was rebuilt methodically through accountability.

If your board received an activist letter tomorrow, could you defend your plan with data and conviction or would you scramble to craft the narrative you should already have told? Are your global risks integrated or scattered across disconnected updates? When crises hit, does your governance default to compliance and defense or can you balance transparency, accountability, and strategy in the same breath?

Public company boards operate in the most unforgiving governance arena. Their challenge is to master the rulebook, engage markets wisely, and build resilience that transcends quarterly scrutiny. Right-sized governance in this context does not just preserve credibility; it preserves the company's license to operate in a global economy where trust can vanish overnight.

The Private Company Board: Freedom with Discipline

Private companies live in the in-between, less regulated than publics, but far more structured than startups. Governance here is personal: owners, families, investors, all sitting at the same table, each with different horizons.

In one family-owned manufacturing group, a founder's daughter and a private-equity partner debated strategy. The founder wanted stability; the investor wanted scale. My board's role wasn't to take sides, it was to translate. They reframed the conversation from *"growth vs. tradition"* to *"legacy through growth."* Governance became mediation in service of continuity.

- **Strategic Growth:** Guiding expansion while protecting founder vision.

- **Succession Planning:** In family businesses, succession is existential. As a Board member, your role is to ensure continuity without complacency.

- **Operational Depth:** Private boards are more hands-on, advising on operations, supply chains, or efficiency gains where the margins for error are slim.

- **M&A Readiness:** Preparing for IPOs, acquisitions, or recapitalizations requires foresight. As Director, you must anticipate not only the transaction itself but also the cultural and structural shifts that follow.

- **Governance Flexibility:** Unlike public boards, structures are often tailored to the owners' preferences. Some boards are advisory and informal; others adopt formal committees that mirror public practices.

Private boards often move faster: fewer committees, more direct dialogue. Meetings feel like strategy workshops, not hearings. But this informality hides risk, especially as companies globalize. Cross-border tax, local labor law, cultural leadership gaps: all need structure.

A mid-sized logistics firm I advised learned this when it opened a European hub. Without a clear delegation of authority, regional leaders made independent supplier deals, exposing the company to regulatory gaps. The fix wasn't punitive, it was procedural: a governance charter defining who decides what, where, and when. Flexibility regained through clarity.

Another family-owned business I worked with had the opportunity to scale into multiple regions and learned that governance had to evolve just as quickly as the business. So, the board created a global governance charter, outlining decision rights across family branches, management teams, and international subsidiaries. This board action not only reduced conflict but also gave external investors' confidence that governance was aligned across borders.

Does your private company board have a plan for succession or is it relying on assumptions that leadership will "figure it out" later? If your enterprise had to expand internationally tomorrow, would your tax, legal, and governance structures hold or would they collapse under local complexity? Is your governance system flexible enough to balance founder vision, family priorities, and investor expectations without gridlock? Do you treat governance as a strategic enabler, or simply as a family obligation?

Private company boards succeed when they embrace their hybrid nature. They are not startups chasing survival, nor public giants battling regulators. They are stewards of growth, legacy, and adaptability. Right-sized governance here means preserving the entrepreneurial spirit while embedding the structures necessary for long-term resilience.

The Non-Profit Board: Mission Before Margin

In non-profits, governance centers on purpose. The compass points toward impact, not financial return. That shift may sound simple, but it changes everything about the board's role. Where corporate directors measure progress in shareholder value, non-profit directors must measure progress in credibility, trust, and mission delivery.

It is tempting to treat non-profit governance as a softer version of corporate oversight. In reality, it can be more demanding. Stakeholder expectations are diffuse, funding streams uncertain, and reputational risk amplified. A misstep in a budget or program may not just cause financial loss, it may erode donor trust, discourage volunteers, and damage the very mission the organization exists to serve.

Key Skills in Non-Profits

- **Fundraising & Philanthropy:** as Directors, you are expected to "give or get." You are not passive overseers; you are ambassadors.

- **Mission Alignment:** Authentic passion is non-negotiable; credibility depends on it.

- **Community Engagement:** as Directors, you lend your credibility to the cause.

- **Compliance:** Transparency and accountability under strict legal and ethical frameworks.

- **Strategic Balance:** Expanding mission without jeopardizing sustainability—growth cannot dilute purpose.

Non-profit boards often rely on volunteerism, which makes them both powerful and vulnerable. Passion fuels engagement, but burnout is real. Reputations are fragile: misuse of funds, even when accidental, can destroy trust overnight. Unlike corporations, where revenue streams can sometimes absorb mistakes, non-profits live on the razor's edge of credibility. One well-documented example is the case of *Feed the Children*, where governance failures and accusations of fund mismanagement in the late 2000s led to leadership upheaval and donor backlash (BoardEffect, *Nonprofit Embezzlement Cases*, 2022). Though the organization ultimately restructured and restored trust, the episode remains a cautionary tale: for non-profits, credibility is not a buffer, it is the business model itself.

When non-profits go global, governance becomes diplomacy. Messaging must travel; compliance must localize. One NGO created a "Global Ethos Statement", a short manifesto capturing shared values across languages and cultures. It guided decisions when policy couldn't.

Does your non-profit board spend enough time managing credibility, not just cash? Do your governance systems protect not only your programs but your reputation for fairness and integrity? If you lifted your non-profit into another cultural context tomorrow, which values would remain constant, and which practices would you adapt? Is that written down?

The Right-Sized Governance Compass

Effective boards tailor their governance to context rather than habit. The **Governance Compass** provides four points—**Clarity, Cadence, Candor, and Calibration**—to help directors right-size oversight and decision-making as organizations grow or evolve.

1. **Clarity** means defining who decides what, when, and with what input. It ensures every director understands the board's true role, whether to advise, approve, or observe and keeps focus on measurable outcomes instead of endless debate.

2. **Cadence** refers to the rhythm of board engagement and information flow. Startups may need fast, frequent touchpoints with lean data; public and private boards function best with quarterly discipline and concise dashboards; non-profits follow program or fundraising cycles. The goal is steady visibility without overwhelming management.

3. **Candor** builds a culture where hard questions are welcome and bad news surfaces early. Healthy boards normalize dissent, ensuring challenge remains constructive, not personal. Transparency becomes a safeguard, not a threat.

4. **Calibration** ensures oversight scales with risk. High-impact areas like AI, acquisitions, or ethics deserve deeper scrutiny, while low-risk innovation should stay nimble. After surprises, the board rebalances tightening control if errors repeat or loosening it when systems prove strong.

Which compass point is weakest in your board today? If you strengthened just that one over the next 90 days, what would change?

Startups vs. Large Corporations: How Each Learns from the Other

This book argues that the best leaders are hybrids, curious enough to move fast and disciplined enough to scale. Chapter 3 showed how startups teach agility; Chapter 4 showed how legacy industries teach resilience. Chapter 5 is where both meet on purpose.

What Corporates Can Learn from Startups

- **Small bets with clear gates.** Pilot → learn → pivot or double down.

- **Customer proximity.** Executives should feel the customer's reality weekly, not quarterly.

- **Bias for action.** Create "decision sprints" where teams bring a recommendation within a week.

- **Ownership culture.** Clear accountability beats diffuse responsibility.

What Startups Can Learn from Corporates

- **Cash discipline.** Liquidity equals survival and opportunity. Educate the whole team on working capital basics.

- **Governance hygiene.** Light-touch policies on data, employment, and contracts save grief later.

- **Scenario planning.** A two-hour tabletop can save you from a two-month crisis.

- **Reputation math.** Treat trust as an asset with compounding returns; protect it early.

Which practice from "the other world" would most help you in the next 90 days and who on your board will champion it?

The Comparative Framework

Board Type	Primary Focus	Key Skills	Differences in Practice	Multinational Complexity
Startup	Growth, funding	Agility, fundraising, GTM, culture	Hands-on, equity-heavy; short cycles	Cross-border fundraising, compliance, distributed teams
Public	Compliance, value	Regulation, risk, capital markets	Process-heavy, liability, scrutiny	Sanctions, multi-jurisdictional reporting, ESG
Private	Strategic growth	Succession, operations, M&A, flexibility	Nimble, owner-aligned	Tax structures, global workforce, family dynamics
Non-Profit	Mission, impact	Fundraising, advocacy, governance	Volunteer energy, public trust	NGO partnerships, multi-lingual messaging

Startup: *Are you over-rotating to vision and under-rotating to cash? What one governance ritual would save you from a preventable failure?*

Public: *What single page would convince an activist to invest rather than attack?*

Private: *If your founder became unavailable tomorrow, who steps in and what would the first 30 days look like?*

Non-Profit: *Are you measuring what donors want and what communities value? Where is trust fragile?*

A Brief Word on Cross-Border Governance

Even small organizations are global faster than they expect remote hires, global suppliers, international customers. Three practical moves:

1. **Map your regulatory surface area** (privacy, labor, tax, sanctions) quarterly.

2. **Localize without fragmenting**—design global standards with local addenda rather than bespoke policies everywhere.

3. **Name a cross-border owner**—someone who keeps a living list of "what it takes to be legal and legitimate" in each market you touch.

If you had to defend your cross-border practices to a skeptical regulator next week, who would speak, what would they show, and how quickly could they assemble it?

Closing Reflection: Stewardship in Motion

Serving on a board is never one-size-fits-all. A startup may need a director who secures funding, recruits a head of sales, and unblocks a distribution deal. A public board must meet the letter of the law and leave space for innovation. A private board balances the founder's spark with systems that outlast any one leader. A non-profit needs ambassadors who protect mission credibility and keep trust visible.

What unites these settings is the essence of governance as stewardship, guiding organizations through uncertainty with the right balance of strategy, empathy, and oversight. Right-sized governance doesn't slow you down; it lets you move faster in the right direction, with fewer surprises and deeper legitimacy.

So let me leave you with a few questions:

- *Is your governance a source of energy or exhaustion?*

- *Where is the smallest intervention that would create the largest improvement?*

- *Who on your board will own the experiment to right-size governance in the next 60 days?*

Right-sized governance gives startups the discipline to scale and gives corporates the agility to innovate without losing control. Boards that master this balance won't just survive disruption; they'll direct it.

Chapter 6

Risk, Ethics, Regulatory and Trust in AI

The story began with a board call scheduled for 7 a.m. A multinational retailer had just discovered that its dynamic pricing algorithm, the one that boosted margins quarter after quarter, was charging higher prices in low-income neighborhoods. The CEO called it a "data anomaly." The headlines called it discrimination.

By noon, regulators were asking questions. By evening, social media had erupted. The board's chair summed up what everyone feared: "We didn't approve that algorithm, but we will be held accountable for it."

That's the new reality of leadership in the algorithmic age. You may not design the code, but you are responsible for what it does.

AI is no longer an innovation story. It is a governance story, one about risk, ethics, and trust. Every time a company deploys AI, it enters into an invisible contract with its employees, customers, and investors: this system will be fair, explainable, and aligned with our values. Break that contract, and no quarterly performance will restore the damage.

AI's greatest challenge is not accuracy, it is accountability. The board's role is to ensure both. Artificial intelligence is not just a tool; it is a trust contract. Every time your organization deploys an algorithm, it makes a silent promise to employees, customers, and shareholders: this system will be fair, safe, and aligned with your values. When that promise is broken through bias, misuse of data, or opaque decision-making, the loss is not only financial. It is reputational, regulatory, and cultural.

In a world where algorithms increasingly shape hiring, lending, healthcare, and justice, trust has become the new currency of leadership. It is earned not through press releases or ethics statements, but through disciplined governance, systems that ensure technology serves people, not the other way around.

Boards and executives must now confront a truth once reserved for safety-critical industries: AI oversight is not only about innovation control, it is about public legitimacy. The more powerful the technology, the more fragile the trust behind it.

A board I once advised learned this the hard way when a seemingly harmless recruitment algorithm began filtering out women from some technical roles. The model had trained on ten years of past hiring data, faithfully replicating the company's historical bias. The result was a digital echo of its own blind spots.

The board was not negligent; it was unaware. But unawareness is no defense. AI doesn't just automate processes, it amplifies values. Every dataset, every objective function becomes a mirror of how a company defines success. One director summarized it bluntly: *"Our algorithms are our ethics at scale."*

Boards must now treat every system that learns, predicts, or decides as a governance artifact, not merely a technical one. The old question was, "Does it work?" The new question is, "What does it optimize for and who pays the price?"

When AI is deployed without moral intention, it will choose efficiency over empathy every time. Ethics is not compliance, it is strategy. Trust is the new currency of leadership.

What human judgment have you replaced and what principles must remain? If your algorithm made tomorrow's front page, would it represent your purpose or betray it? Are you governing AI as a tool for scale or as a mirror of your company's values?

In the pages ahead, you'll see how ethics, risk, and trust intersect not as abstract ideals but as the foundation of competitive advantage. We'll explore how boards can turn principles into measurable systems, how to navigate emerging regulations across continents, and how to translate frameworks like NIST's AI Risk Management into boardroom action. By the end of this chapter, you'll not only recognize AI oversight as a fiduciary responsibility, you'll know how to lead it with clarity, confidence, and credibility.

The Four Dimensions of AI Risk

Boards are fluent in risk. They understand operational, reputational, and financial exposure instinctively. AI does not replace these categories, it compresses them, accelerates their impact, and introduces a fourth dimension that boards are still learning to govern: autonomy risk. The risk of decisions made faster than governance can react.

Operational Risk — Speed Without Supervision

A few years ago, a logistics company I advised in its AI rollout faced a challenge none of its dashboards had predicted. They had deployed an AI routing system to cut fuel costs and delivery times. On paper, it was a success story, KPIs were green across the board. But field reports started telling a different story: drivers were being sent through unsafe neighborhoods at night, all because the algorithm prioritized the shortest route. The model optimized distance, not danger.

This is operational risk in the AI age: systems that act faster than humans can intervene. Directors must ensure that efficiency is never mistaken for resilience. Governance frameworks should set "ethical guardrails", the red lines beyond which automation cannot go.

If a system can act faster than governance can intervene, governance must be redesigned.

Reputational Risk — Fairness as a Business Asset

Reputational risk is where AI failures become public often suddenly, and often irreversibly.

I first encountered this when reading a headline about a major financial services firm whose automated underwriting system was quietly rejecting qualified minority applicants. The story, widely covered in several reputable publications, revealed how an algorithm trained on historical data was systematically disadvantaging certain borrower demographics. What caught my attention wasn't just the technology, it was the boardroom reaction: a crisis of trust, not just a technical glitch. That media story reminded me that oversight failures aren't always dramatic—they often begin with metrics that look fine until someone raises the question: "Who's checking this?" Boards don't need to debug the code, but they do need to ask what the algorithm is optimizing for—and who might lose if it's wrong.

Fairness is no longer an act of corporate virtue; it is a commercial necessity. Reputation, once lost, becomes a governance liability. If fairness is not explicitly governed, reputation will eventually be regulated by headlines.

Financial Risk — When Algorithms Move Capital, Not Just Data

Financial risk deserves explicit treatment because AI increasingly moves money directly. Dynamic pricing, credit approval, fraud detection, inventory optimization, and automated trading systems all convert algorithmic decisions into immediate financial outcomes. When they fail, losses are beyond theoretical, they hit margins, valuations, and balance sheets.

The retailer described at the beginning of this chapter learned this the hard way. Its pricing algorithm boosted margins for quarters until discriminatory outcomes triggered regulatory scrutiny, customer backlash, and forced pricing rollbacks. What looked like an ethics issue quickly became a material financial event.

Financial risk also appears indirectly in regulatory fines, litigation exposure, increased cost of capital and valuation discounts due to trust erosion

If AI decisions affect pricing, credit, employment, or access, they are financial controls and must be governed as such.

Autonomy Risk — When Decisions Outpace Governance

Autonomy risk is the most misunderstood and most dangerous dimension. It arises when AI systems learn continuously, adapt without reapproval, act at scale and make decisions humans no longer fully understand in real time

This is not about malicious AI, it is about delegated authority without updated accountability.

Boards often ask, "Is the model accurate?" The better question is, "How much authority have we delegated and can we pull it back?"

Autonomy risk explains why:

- Small model updates trigger large public consequences
- Failures surprise leadership
- Boards say, "We didn't approve that decision but we own it"

Every AI system needs a clearly defined decision boundary considering what it may decide, escalate, or never do alone.

Autonomy risk does not remain internal for long. When algorithms make decisions faster than governance can intervene, the consequences rarely stop at operational surprises or internal post-mortems. They spill outward into regulators' offices, courtrooms, investor calls, and public discourse.

This is the inflection point where internal governance failures become external accountability. Regulators step in not because companies used AI, but because they failed to govern its autonomy responsibly. And competitors gain advantage not because they took fewer risks, but because they built governance systems that allowed them to move faster *with* confidence.

In other words, autonomy risk is the bridge between how AI behaves inside your organization and how the world responds to it. From here, two forces shape outcomes beyond your control: regulation and strategy.

Regulatory Risk — The Coming Global Convergence

According to the European Union's AI Act, AI systems are classified into four risk tiers (unacceptable, high, limited, and minimal), with non-compliance penalties reaching up to 7% of a company's global annual turnover.

In the U.S., the Federal Trade Commission (FTC) warns that "automation bias" and unverified claims will be treated as deceptive trade practices. China's Algorithmic Regulation requires registration and transparency for recommendation systems.

And the Organization for Economic Co-operation and Development (OECD) and United Nations Educational,

Scientific and Cultural Organization (UNESCO) frameworks now guide dozens of nations toward principles of accountability and human oversight.

For boards, this means AI governance must evolve from "policy language" to structured accountability: clear ownership, documentation, and audit trails for every high-impact model.

Regulators no longer accept ignorance as innocence.

Strategic Risk — When Fear Blocks Innovation

Not all risk comes from misuse; some comes from avoidance. I remember a case which one energy company froze its AI program after early bias concerns. Meanwhile, competitors integrated predictive models into maintenance, saving millions and improving safety.

The result: one company lost trust by acting too fast; another lost relevance by acting too slow. Governance, therefore, must navigate between reckless speed and paralyzing caution balancing innovation with integrity.

Boards can transform ethical aspiration into operational clarity through a Trust Framework built around three enduring principles — Transparency, Fairness, and Accountability — anchored by a fourth, often overlooked element: Proportionality.

- **Transparency** — Can decisions be explained in plain language to directors, regulators, and customers?

- **Fairness** — Are outcomes demonstrably unbiased and auditable across demographics and contexts?

- **Accountability** — Is there a clearly named owner when things go wrong, and a process for remediation?

- **Proportionality** — Are governance controls matched to the risk and potential impact of each system?

This framework reflects the philosophy behind the NIST AI Risk Management Framework (RMF) to map, measure, manage, and govern AI risk according to context and consequence.

Boards should demand alignment with such frameworks—not as bureaucracy, but as a common language of trust between technologists, regulators, and society.

I recall how one director in a manufacturing conglomerate put it this way: "We learned to audit financials line by line; now we must learn to audit algorithms by intent."

Are your board's AI oversight tools scaled to the actual risk of each system, or are they blanket policies that create blind spots? When your AI models act faster than governance can respond, what safeguards ensure they never act beyond your values? Do your board packs translate AI risk into business impact or just technical jargon? Is accountability for AI decisions explicit, documented, and auditable?

Ethics as Strategy, Not Compliance

Compliance answers the letter of the law. Strategy answers the spirit of leadership. Ethics in AI is not about avoiding trouble; it is about earning trust, the currency that buys future opportunity. Too many boards still treat ethics as compliance, a checklist to satisfy regulators or investor questionnaires. Yet ethical AI is not a constraint on innovation; it is a competitive advantage.

I remember reading a case that caught my attention during the height of AI adoption in healthcare. A large health network had deployed an AI system to optimize appointment scheduling. On paper, it was a success as clinics were running at near-full capacity, efficiency metrics looked great, and administrators celebrated reduced idle time. But then, patient satisfaction began to plummet. The algorithm had optimized throughput, not care continuity. Patients were seeing different doctors each visit, and clinicians felt the growing pressure of relentless scheduling.

That story stayed with me because it perfectly illustrated a boardroom dilemma I've seen across sectors: when efficiency metrics outpace human values. After public criticism and an internal review, the health network reset its definition of success, prioritizing continuity of care, reduced no-shows, and better patient feedback. The same AI, retrained under new parameters, ultimately improved both outcomes and morale.

It was a clear reminder that technology amplifies whatever values we encode into it. If you measure only for speed and cost, that's all you'll get. But if you embed trust, empathy, and purpose into your design, AI becomes a force for both performance and humanity.

The insight: ethics is a design choice. What you optimize defines who you are.

In a very well-known case, a global technology company voluntarily exited its general-purpose facial recognition business, citing risks of misuse and civil-rights violations. At the time, investors questioned the decision and analysts criticized the immediate loss of revenue. But as public scrutiny of surveillance technologies intensified, that early restraint became a strategic asset. Regulators viewed the company as a responsible actor rather than a reluctant one, civil-society groups publicly shifted their tone from skepticism to cautious trust, and enterprise customers began citing the move as evidence of ethical maturity. By stepping back before being forced to, the company didn't simply avoid risk, it regained credibility as a leader willing to prioritize long-term trust over short-term gains.

Ethics serve as a powerful talent magnet, attracting professionals who seek purpose, trust, and integrity in the organizations they choose to join. Boards often overlook one of AI ethics' most practical dividends: talent retention. Engineers today want to build products that make them proud. When boards treat ethics as strategic, with visible commitments and public principles, companies attract the best minds, who see values as a competitive edge.

As one chief scientist told me, "I can teach a machine to learn, but I want to work for a company that learns ethically." His point was unmistakable: technical brilliance means nothing if the organization surrounding it cannot exercise judgment, humility, and accountability. For you as a leader or board member, this quote is a reminder that talent chooses cultures, not just companies. The people capable of building your most powerful systems will only stay if they trust the values guiding them. Ethical learning is not a slogan; it is a competitive advantage.

The Boardroom Risk Compass (Based on NIST AI RMF)

To translate principles into practice, boards need a risk compass — adapted from the NIST AI Risk Management Framework (RMF). The NIST model is structured around four key actions: Govern, Map, Measure, and Manage. In the boardroom, they become the leadership cycle of Stewardship, Context, Measurement, and Action.

Stewardship — Governance with Intent

Every AI initiative begins with purpose. Boards should insist that each system explicitly state:

- What problem it solves
- What objective function it optimizes
- What ethical constraints it must obey

For example, at a large industrial company, the board required that each algorithmic project include an "Ethical Purpose Statement." That one-page summary, signed by both the product owner and a director, listed the intended benefits, potential harm, and oversight mechanisms.

The document didn't slow innovation; it sharpened it. Teams worked faster because intent was clear.

Who in your organization signs off on ethical intent? Does every major system have a documented "human in command"?

Context — Understanding Impact and Ecosystem

AI's influence extends far beyond technical boundaries. Boards must assess who and what each system touches.

During the pandemic, a consumer app once discovered its recommendation engine was spreading health misinformation. It had not been designed maliciously, only carelessly. The board responded with an "Impact Mapping" tool: for every project, teams now list all affected stakeholders, downstream dependencies, and social sensitivities.

Context isn't bureaucracy, it's foresight. Have we mapped potential harm outside our four walls? Who has authority to stop deployment if risk exceeds tolerance?

Measurement — Making Ethics Quantifiable

You can't manage what you don't measure including fairness and transparency. Boards should require dashboards that track:

- Bias detection and remediation frequency
- Model drift incidents

- Explainability ratings
- Human override counts
- Stakeholder trust surveys

I came across an insightful case in the financial sector that I still reference often. A leading bank began publishing an AI Ethics Scorecard to its board every quarter, measuring transparency, bias testing, and human oversight across all deployed models. The impact was immediate and accountability became part of the culture. Managers who once hid behind technical complexity began competing for better transparency scores, treating ethics as performance, not paperwork. What struck me most was how a simple governance tool turned aspiration into evidence: when you measure trust, it starts to grow.

Does your board receive AI risk metrics alongside financial KPIs? Can management explain a model failure in one slide without jargon?

Action — Evolve with Learning

AI evolves continuously; governance must too. Every model failure should lead to a post-mortem and framework update, just as safety incidents reshape industrial procedures.

During a governance roundtable, a case was shared that perfectly captured what proactive oversight looks like in practice. A global manufacturer had set up an AI Resilience Committee reporting to its audit chair, an unusual step at the time. Each quarter, the committee simulated a model failure: a data breach, a bias exposure, or an automation gone wrong. Every incident was treated as a rehearsal, not a crisis. Within a year, their response time was cut in half, and stakeholder confidence had noticeably improved. The story stuck with me because it proved that resilience isn't about having perfect systems, it's about building the reflex to recover fast and transparently when things fail.

Adaptability is the essence of responsible innovation.

When was your last AI incident simulation? How do lessons learned update board policy in real time?

Building an Ethical Risk Framework

Boards need a clear reference point. Below is a synthesis of the NIST AI RMF, OECD AI Principles, and ISO/IEC 42001 guidelines — tailored for directors. Readers should use this section as a practical checklist and discussion tool to assess their organization's current practices, identify governance gaps, and guide informed, values-aligned boardroom decisions.

Dimension	Board-Level Focus	Illustrative Practices
Transparency	Ensure systems are explainable to non-technical stakeholders.	Plain-language summaries, model documentation ("model cards"), public disclosure for high-impact AI.
Fairness	Prevent systemic bias and discriminatory outcomes.	Regular bias audits, diverse data governance teams, external reviews.
Accountability	Assign ownership for each AI decision path.	Named executives for model performance and ethics; board-level AI oversight committee.
Security & Resilience	Protect systems against manipulation and data poisoning.	Penetration testing, data provenance audits, secure model retraining pipelines.
Human Oversight	Maintain meaningful human control and intervention capability.	"Human-in-command" policies, override rights, red-team testing.
Adaptability	Evolve governance with technology and regulation.	Annual framework refresh, training, and independent assessment.

The lesson: AI governance is not static, it's a living system.

Trust as the New Currency of Leadership

Trust can no longer be treated as intangible. It is a measurable asset and a multiplier of enterprise value.

During a recent crisis, two similar fintech firms faced data breaches. One hid the event; the other live-streamed its response, issued customer updates hourly, and published a post-mortem. Both lost data. Only one lost trust.

Investors later rewarded the transparent firm with higher valuation and lower customer churn. The difference wasn't cybersecurity; it was governance transparency.

Another grate example is a global manufacturer which the CEO began quarterly "Ethics Town Halls," where engineers presented not only their successes but the ethical dilemmas they faced. Employees saw that moral judgment wasn't punished, it was rewarded. Engagement soared.

The result? Lower turnover, faster innovation, and improved customer satisfaction. Trust created velocity.

The Regulatory Horizon: From Fragmentation to Global Accountability

When the CFO of a multinational asked during a board meeting, "Which AI laws apply to us?" the silence was telling. The general counsel finally said, "All of them and none of them clearly."

That confusion is becoming universal. AI regulation is arriving not as a single code but as a global mosaic fragmented, overlapping, and rapidly tightening. Boards that treat regulation as an afterthought will soon discover it's a strategic frontier.

In this new patchwork of accountability, the EU AI Act is the most comprehensive, dividing AI into risk categories—unacceptable, high, limited, and minimal—and imposing compliance obligations across the entire value chain. High-risk systems (like hiring, credit, or healthcare AI) must meet strict documentation, human oversight, and transparency standards, with penalties reaching 7% of global revenue.

In the U.S., there is no federal AI law yet. But the Federal Trade Commission (FTC) has asserted jurisdiction over deceptive or discriminatory AI practices, warning that "you can't escape accountability just because your algorithm made the call." State-level momentum from California's privacy laws to Colorado's AI fairness act adds layers of complexity.

Across Asia, Singapore's AI Verify, Japan's AI Governance Guidelines, and China's Algorithmic Recommendation Provisions create regional variations: some emphasize innovation sandboxes, others strict data control. Canada's Artificial Intelligence and Data Act (AIDA) introduces a new "accountable AI officer" role.

Across Latin America, regulations are shifting from principle to practice. Brazil leads the region with its draft Artificial Intelligence Bill, a risk-based framework aligned with the EU AI Act and OECD principles, combining state oversight with industry self-regulation under the supervision of the National Data Protection Authority (ANPD). The proposal builds on the LGPD privacy law, linking data ethics with algorithmic accountability. In Latin America, ethical innovation is emerging as both a regulatory expectation and a competitive advantage.

For boards operating across these markets, compliance means more than avoiding penalties, it demands cultural legitimacy and visible commitment to social impact. For boards, this patchwork is more than legal noise, it's a map of moral expectations.

I recall a case which a global energy company deployed predictive maintenance AI across Europe, Asia, and the U.S. Each region had its own rules: data localization in Asia, transparency reports in Europe, voluntary ethics statements in the U.S.

During an incident review, auditors found the model had used unapproved third-party telemetry data from a supplier in one jurisdiction. No harm occurred—but the noncompliance triggered a cascade: EU regulators demanded proof of data provenance; Asian partners suspended data sharing; U.S. investors questioned oversight.

The problem wasn't misconduct, it was misalignment. The board responded by forming an AI Compliance Council, uniting legal, data, and business leaders. They adopted the NIST AI Risk Management Framework as the company's global baseline, cross-referencing it with ISO/IEC 42001 standards for accountability, documentation, and continuous improvement.

Within a year, the company wasn't just compliant, it was credible. It moved from reacting to regulation to shaping it, participating in policy dialogues and setting internal precedents others followed.

The boards that will thrive in this new regulatory environment won't merely meet minimum standards; they'll institutionalize transparency and anticipate change. They'll view compliance not as a burden but as a competitive differentiator, proof that their AI systems are safe, explainable, and human-centered.

Forward-looking directors now demand:

- Regulatory readiness reports at each audit cycle.
- Cross-border AI impact mapping (who regulates what).
- Scenario testing for new AI laws (e.g., simulate EU high-risk classification).

- Continuous horizon scanning, tied to ethics and ESG committees.

As one chairperson put it, "If regulation is coming anyway, let's lead it, not fear it."

Does your board track upcoming AI legislation by region and industry? Who in your company is responsible for interpreting and harmonizing these frameworks? Are you designing AI governance to meet regulations or to shape it? If your company were audited tomorrow under the EU AI Act or NIST RMF, could you produce the evidence regulators would expect?

The Global Perspective

Across regions, the nature of trust varies but the need for it does not.

- In Europe, trust is compliance credibility under GDPR and the EU AI Act.
- In Asia, it's relational harmony and long-term respect.
- In North America, it's transparency and accountability.
- In Latin America and Africa, it's fairness and social stewardship.

Global boards must localize their approach but unify their intent. The language of trust is cultural; the principle of accountability is universal.

From Risk to Resilience: The Board's Role Ahead

The future boardroom will not ask, *"Should we use AI?"* but *"Are we governing it wisely?"* That distinction determines whether AI becomes an accelerator of trust or a source of existential risk.

A multinational learned this after its chatbot, designed to cut support calls, began spreading misinformation following a data update. Screenshots went viral. "We treated it as a technology problem," one director admitted later. "It was a governance problem." The company responded with an AI Ethics Charter, quarterly model reviews, and staff workshops on algorithmic literacy. Within a year, customer trust exceeded pre-crisis levels. That is governance evolution: from panic to preparedness.

Boards that wish to replicate that success can use the Governance Compass described in chapter 5 with four questions that anchor AI oversight without bureaucracy:

1. **Clarity:** Who decides what, by when, and with which data?
2. **Cadence:** Are reporting rhythms aligned to system velocity?
3. **Candor:** Are failures surfaced early without fear?
4. **Calibration:** Are controls adjusted to actual risk and business impact?

Each principle reflects a balance: not too much control to kill speed, not too little to lose sight. Strengthen even one compass point, and your board will move from reactive compliance to confident oversight.

Which compass point—clarity, cadence, candor, or calibration—is weakest in your AI oversight? How would your governance rhythm change if AI were treated as both a risk and an opportunity engine?

Designing for Trust — The Board's Challenge Ahead

The most consequential technologies rarely arrive with fanfare. They appear as defaults—the model that screens résumés, the price that updates itself, the safety alert that no one questions because it came from "the algorithm."

Governance is the discipline of making the invisible visible of aligning technology with purpose before crisis makes the headlines.

Directors don't need to code. But they must ask the harder questions: the ones not answered by enthusiasm, the ones that demand clarity over convenience. Hold the line on proportional risk, human dignity, and public trust, and AI becomes a multiplier of mission not a threat to legitimacy.

When the next test comes, and it will, will your stakeholders see a company that uses AI with speed *and* integrity, or one that lets speed decide for them?

In the end, governance is not a brake on innovation, it is the architecture of trust that lets organizations run fast without running blind. In tomorrow's boardrooms, that trust will not only be your greatest technology, but it will also be your legacy.

Closing Reflection

Trust is not a soft value; it is a measurable asset. In the age of algorithms, it determines which companies earn loyalty, attract talent, and secure regulatory goodwill. Boards that treat AI ethics as strategy, not compliance, will find that trust compounds like capital. It builds credibility in markets where scrutiny is rising and expectations are relentless.

AI risk management is not about predicting every failure, it's about building systems that can explain, recover, and learn from them. The frameworks may evolve, the regulations may differ by region, but one constant remains: accountability is the currency of legitimacy. The most advanced models in the world are worthless without the confidence of the people who use them.

So, as you close this chapter, ask yourself: *If an AI failure strikes your organization tomorrow, would your board be ready to explain, to act, and to rebuild trust? Or would you still be drafting a policy while the headlines write themselves?*

Because in the end, governing AI isn't about controlling technology, it's about earning the right to use it. The future belongs to the boards that can do both.

Chapter 7

Global Adaptability as a Strategic Edge

The World as a Boardroom

Have you ever made a costly assumption when expanding into another country? Maybe your company launched a product that failed to resonate with local consumers—or entered a market confident in its global strategy, only to discover that culture, regulation, and pace rewrote the rules. Most leaders have. Global expansion humbles even the most experienced executives, revealing that what worked brilliantly in one country can falter, sometimes spectacularly, in another.

The world no longer transforms in unison; it shifts in fragments. Technology accelerates at different speeds, regulations collide, and geopolitics redraw the map faster than strategy decks can catch up. For today's boards, global adaptability is no longer optional, it's the heartbeat of transformation.

Global adaptability isn't about being everywhere, it's about understanding everywhere. It's the ability to read context as fluently as you read financials, to sense that transformation wears a different face in every market. What works in Houston may falter in Hamburg; what inspires in São Paulo may confuse in Singapore. And what passes as innovation in Silicon Valley may trigger a national-security debate in Brussels or Beijing. The future belongs not to those who expand the fastest, but to those who listen the deepest—to cultures, to regulators, to customers whose definitions of progress diverge as much as their languages.

True global adaptability demands a dual lens: a global mindset and a local understanding. It means connecting strategy to culture, and ambition to nuance. The boardroom must think globally, anticipating geopolitical shifts, regulatory currents, and cross-border risks, while empowering teams to act locally, designing solutions that fit human realities on the ground. The most effective leaders I've seen aren't just globally mobile, they're globally perceptive. They know when to scale a model and when to rewrite it, when to lead with efficiency and when to lead with empathy.

Board transformation, therefore, isn't just about adopting new technologies; it's about navigating the geopolitical and cultural currents that shape them. Supply-chain realignments, data-sovereignty laws, and regional conflicts now influence corporate strategy as much as market forces or consumer behavior. A board that fails to interpret these shifts risks being strategically right, but globally irrelevant.

So, as you read this chapter, ask yourself: *how fluent are you in local context? When was the last time your global strategy truly reflected regional insight rather than corporate instinct? Does your organization's strategy adapt to different cultural and regulatory contexts or assume one size fits all? How well does your board anticipate geopolitical shifts that could reshape supply, data, or talent flows? Do you have voices around the table who can translate between markets between speed and caution, scale and sensitivity?*

This chapter is designed to make you a more effective leader across borders. It will help you anticipate where strategies break down as they travel, spot risks before they become reputational or regulatory crises, and adapt transformation without diluting purpose. You'll learn how cultural intelligence, regulatory foresight, and diverse leadership translate into better board decisions in real markets not theory. Through practical examples drawn from five continents, this chapter shows how globally adaptable leaders build resilience and momentum by learning faster than change moves, rather than trying to control it.

In a world where disruption moves at different speeds, adaptability across cultures and systems is the ultimate differentiator of leadership.

Why Adaptability Defines Future Leadership

Artificial intelligence, sustainability, digital transformation, these are global conversations. Yet every region joins them in its own dialect. Boards often assume technology will create convergence. The opposite is true: technology exposes divergence. The same AI model or data governance framework that delivers value in the U.S. may spark controversy in Europe or stall in Asia under different regulations or social expectations.

Adaptability is more than a leadership trait, it's the connective tissue linking strategy, culture, and execution across borders. Global adaptability means more than operating in multiple markets; it means understanding them deeply. It's the capacity to navigate the intersection of innovation, regulation, and culture to turn complexity into coherence. Future-ready leaders must learn to read the world like a map of shifting contexts, not a single narrative. Leaders of the future will not simply export best practices—they will translate them.

The next generation of directors will not ask, "Are we a startup or a legacy company?" but "*How do we combine the agility of a startup with the discipline of a legacy system and make it work globally?*" This is what I call strategic elasticity: the ability to adapt without losing alignment. Leaders who master it recognize that a policy in Brussels, a tariff in Washington, or a data law in São Paulo can redefine global value chains overnight.

Adaptability is not a "soft" skill; it is a strategic competency. It defines how organizations survive global turbulence, whether through pandemics, political shifts, or technological disruption. Yet it also demands emotional and cultural intelligence, the awareness that what resonates in one market might fail in another.

So, *does your leadership team reflect true global fluency, not just global presence? When your board debates transformation, do you weigh local nuance as carefully as financial return?* In a world where disruption moves at different speeds, adaptability across cultures and systems is the ultimate differentiator of leadership.

Regional Contrasts: Five Speeds of Disruption

United States – Innovation as Identity

In the United States, disruption is not feared, it's celebrated. The culture of innovation is steeped in optimism and reinvention, born from a national narrative that rewards risk-takers. "Fail fast" is not just a slogan; it's a badge of courage. In Silicon Valley boardrooms, speed is often substituted for certainty. The assumption is that the market will forgive mistakes if learning is fast enough. Startups pivot in weeks; corporations emulate entrepreneurial behaviors to stay relevant.

Yet the American strength—velocity—can also become a liability. The obsession with growth can lead to oversight gaps, particularly around ethics and sustainability. I recall one technology board where a director confessed, "We never stopped to ask whether we should, only how fast we could." That's the American paradox: innovation as both fuel and fire. Boards that balance ambition with accountability turn that volatility into advantage.

For directors operating in U.S. contexts, the governance challenge is not how to slow innovation, but how to anchor it, how to build moral guardrails that allow speed without recklessness. The most effective leaders in this environment don't resist disruption; they choreograph it.

Europe – Regulation as Reputation

In Europe, disruption wears a different face. Here, progress is measured not by speed but by stability. Privacy, safety, and ethics are not compliance afterthoughts, they are cultural imperatives. Citizens expect governance as a form of protection, not constraint. The EU's leadership in sustainability, digital privacy (GDPR), and the upcoming AI Act reflects this mindset: innovation must serve society before shareholders.

I remember a board meeting in Brussels where a CEO announced a delay in launching a new predictive analytics product due to data compliance concerns. Instead of frustration, the board applauded. The delay was seen not as failure but as foresight. That moment crystallized the European ethos: integrity before impact.

For boards leading in or into Europe, the lesson is clear, trust precedes technology. Companies that rush to scale without ethical validation may win short-term gains but lose long-term legitimacy. The European market rewards patience, transparency, and respect for privacy. And increasingly, global investors are watching how European governance norms are influencing boardrooms elsewhere.

Asia – Scale and Speed as Strategy

Asia moves at a tempo the rest of the world struggles to match. From Singapore's digital infrastructure to South Korea's 5G ecosystems and China's AI dominance, progress is orchestrated at national scale. Speed is not chaos, it's choreography. Government, industry, and academia often align around shared national visions, compressing innovation cycles that take years elsewhere into months.

But this efficiency comes with cultural nuance. In Asia, decision-making is often consensus driven. Patience precedes precision. Relationships and hierarchy matter as much as results. I once worked with a Japanese partner who paused a multimillion-dollar decision to "let harmony settle." It felt slow until I realized that the pause built unity, not delay. Once consensus formed, execution was flawless.

For boards expanding into Asia, the challenge is to move fast with respect. Western leaders sometimes make mistakes in deliberation for hesitation. In reality, it's strategic patience—an investment in trust. The leaders who thrive in Asia learn that agility here isn't about disruption, it's about disciplined alignment.

Latin America – Disruption Born of Necessity

In Latin America, disruption often begins not in labs but in communities. Economic volatility, political shifts, and infrastructure gaps make innovation a matter of survival. Here, resilience is not a buzzword, it's daily practice. When capital is scarce, creativity becomes currency.

I once analyzed a startup in South America developing an AI system for predicting bus arrivals. Their data sources? WhatsApp messages from riders and informal driver networks. It wasn't elegant, but it worked and it served millions. The founders stated, "We couldn't wait for perfect data; we built trust first, and the tech followed." That is Latin American ingenuity at its finest; innovation grounded in empathy.

Boards operating in Latin America must embrace flexibility and humility. Strategies designed for predictability collapse under volatility. Success here depends on empowering local leadership, fostering partnerships, and measuring progress not only in profit but in resilience. The region teaches that disruption is not about breaking systems; it's about rebuilding them in real time.

Africa – Leapfrogging Toward the Future

Africa's innovation story defies linear development. Freed from legacy infrastructure, many nations have leapt directly into the digital age. The rise of M-Pesa in Kenya turned mobile phones into banks long before Western fintechs imagined it. Across the continent, entrepreneurs use technology to solve fundamental challenges, energy access, healthcare logistics, agricultural transparency, with creativity born from constraint.

In one project I observed in West Africa, a renewable energy startup used AI to predict microgrid performance in rural villages. Their challenge wasn't technology, it was trust. Villagers wanted proof that systems would last beyond pilot programs. When the company created a local governance committee composed of community leaders, adoption doubled. The lesson? Innovation without inclusion stalls.

For global boards, Africa offers a profound message: progress need not follow the path of predecessors. It can leap. It can be reimagined. It can redefine efficiency, trust, and impact from the ground up. To engage effectively, leaders must replace the lens of "emerging markets" with "emerging models." Africa doesn't just need investment, it offers inspiration.

Across continents, the rhythms of disruption differ but the melody is the same: trust, adaptation, and context.

Boards that govern globally must play all five tempos at once, fast in innovation, firm in integrity, flexible in culture, faithful to purpose, and fearless in complexity.

Which rhythm dominates your boardroom, speed, caution, consensus, or resilience? How do you adapt your governance cadence when entering a new market? Do you have directors who can translate between these worlds not just linguistically, but strategically?

I remember following a renewable energy venture that began in South Asia with a simple but audacious idea: turning agricultural waste into electricity for villages far from the grid. The founders weren't backed by vast capital or government support. What they had was ingenuity and a deep understanding of local realities. Their first prototypes were built from scrap machinery; their first customers paid in small installments because that was the only viable model in communities without formal banking.

The system worked. Villages lit up for the first time, small businesses thrived, and the company gained recognition as a model for rural electrification. But when they tried to scale the same model in Africa, it almost collapsed. Local supply chains, financing structures, and regulatory frameworks were entirely different. What had succeeded in India failed in Nigeria.

That's where the leadership's real transformation began. Instead of forcing one model across continents, the board treated each market as a learning lab. In East Africa, they shifted from biomass to solar-hybrid microgrids, partnered with community cooperatives, and restructured financing to include pay-as-you-go options. They learned that adaptability wasn't about copying success, it was about re-engineering trust, partnerships, and governance for each new environment.

I didn't advise the company directly, but I remember discussing it with another board director who admired their turnaround. What impressed both of us wasn't the technology, it was the discipline. Every market entry began with a stakeholder audit, a social-impact baseline, and predefined exit triggers. The company's "global expansion plan" became a case study in humility and recalibration.

Today, their model powers hundreds of communities across Asia and Africa. Not because they grew fast, but because they learned how to grow differently. In a world where expansion often means exporting assumptions, this company thrived by exporting empathy and importing understanding.

For me, that's the essence of global adaptability: the courage to test your convictions in unfamiliar terrain and the wisdom to rebuild them when context changes.

The lesson for boards? Transformation succeeds when it fits local reality, not when it follows global trends.

In your Board discussions, *how much time do you talk about global adaptability to the company initiatives? Does your organization assume disruption moves at one speed? Are you testing global strategies against local expectations? When entering new markets, do you listen first or lead with assumptions?*

The Adaptability Gap: Lessons from Global Leadership

Too many companies assume success at home guarantees success abroad. But expansion is not replication, it's reinvention.

Once discussed with a fellow board member the story of a European energy company that expanded its operations into Asia, bringing along its celebrated "zero-incident" safety program. In Europe, the system was a point of pride, rooted in strong labor standards, collective agreements, and a shared culture of procedural discipline. But when applied in Asia, the same framework struggled. Workers saw it as bureaucratic and foreign, something imposed rather than owned. Engagement lagged, and the safety culture the company was known for simply didn't take hold.

What changed wasn't the documentation or the metrics, it was the mindset. The company reframed the initiative not around compliance, but around community safety, emphasizing family well-being, mutual accountability, and local relevance. Suddenly, participation surged. Crews began adapting procedures to fit real working conditions, and local leaders took ownership.

When I heard the story, it resonated deeply. I've seen how even the best-intentioned global strategies can falter when they fail to translate purpose across cultures. It's a reminder that adaptability in governance isn't about yielding. it's about connecting. It's about recognizing that the same value, expressed through a different cultural lens, can multiply trust rather than dilute it.

Adaptability is not compromise; it's alignment. It's the ability to translate vision without losing intent. Boards that mistake uniformity for consistency create resistance. Adaptability doesn't dilute culture—it scales it responsibly.

Across five continents, I've seen how leadership expectations shift with geography.

In Asia, leaders earn respect through patience and listening. Decisions take time but once made, execution is fast. In Europe, rigor and transparency build trust. Governance precedes growth. In Latin America, warmth and relationships come before deals; loyalty sustains performance. In the Middle East, hierarchy still defines order, but hospitality defines respect. And in the United States, leaders are expected to act decisively, visibly, and fast.

I once led an industrial project spanning the U.S., Europe, and West Africa. The European team demanded detailed risk analysis. The Americans pushed for immediate action. The African team asked first about community impact. The only way forward was synthesis, acknowledging that each team's perspective was right within its context.

Leadership, I realized, is translation with empathy. It's not about changing your principles; it's about expressing them in a way people can hear.

Adaptability as a Leadership Skill

In the context of global adaptability, leadership is no longer about commanding stability, it's about orchestrating flexibility with purpose. To lead effectively across borders, directors and executives must develop a global mindset: the ability to think globally while acting locally, aligning strategy with the unique cultural, regulatory, and operational realities of each market.

Global adaptability, at its core, means translating vision into context, knowing when to standardize and when to localize, when to assert discipline and when to invite innovation. It demands three interlocking intelligences: cultural intelligence to understand how values and behaviors vary across regions; regulatory intelligence to anticipate shifting laws and geopolitical undercurrents; and talent intelligence to build diverse, empowered teams that reflect the world they serve. Together, these intelligences form the operating system of future-ready leadership, one capable of steering organizations through disruption without losing coherence or integrity.

1. Cultural Intelligence

Understanding how norms, values, and motivations shape business behavior. A retail company learned this when expanding to Japan. Its Western-style self-checkout kiosks initially failed because customers felt awkward scanning their own goods, cultural etiquette favored human service. The company succeeded only after blending technology with tradition: automated checkout stations staffed by polite attendants who guided the process.

Lesson: Cultural intelligence doesn't reject innovation; it refines it.

2. Regulatory Intelligence

Anticipating global shifts in digital, AI, and sustainability laws. Boards that once saw regulation as a constraint now treat it as strategic foresight. A multinational industrial group created a "Regulatory Radar" dashboard mapping over 50 jurisdictions, aligning AI and data initiatives with emerging laws before they became mandates. When the EU AI Act passed, the company was already compliant.

Lesson: Governance agility is a competitive moat.

3. Talent Intelligence

Building leadership teams that reflect the diversity of the markets they serve. Diverse teams don't just avoid blind spots, they expand opportunity.

I once heard the story of a global consumer brand that decided to reimagine its board composition to reflect the markets it served. For years, decisions about products, marketing, and strategy were made almost entirely from headquarters in Europe. As the company expanded into Asia, Africa, and Latin America, it encountered subtle but costly missteps: a color that carried the wrong meaning in one region, a slogan that fell flat in another, and a "global campaign" that resonated in Paris but puzzled customers in São Paulo. Realizing the limits of its perspective, the board acted decisively, it added independent directors from four continents, each bringing not only market insight but lived cultural context.

Within a year, the transformation was visible. Product teams began testing fragrances inspired by regional preferences, packaging reflected local aesthetics, and brand storytelling celebrated cultural diversity instead of simply translating Western ideas. The company entered six new markets, tripled its culturally tailored portfolio, and achieved double-digit growth in regions where it had once struggled. What struck me most, when I later discussed the case with another director, was the shift in mindset. The board stopped seeing globalization as replication and started treating it as conversation. It learned that diversity at the table isn't a formality, it's a governance advantage.

What this company learned is something every board must eventually face: diversity at the table isn't a gesture, it's a governance strategy. When cultural intelligence meets corporate discipline, the organization doesn't just operate globally, it thinks globally.

When you reflect about your company or your board, who in your organization acts as your cultural interpreter? Do your KPIs reward global insight or local imitation? How often does your leadership test ideas with cross-border teams before execution?

Lesson: Talent intelligence builds teams that learn fast and adapt even faster.

Global Collaboration for AI Governance

We are entering an era where AI governance is the new diplomacy. AI has made governance global by necessity. Data crosses borders faster than regulation can follow. No single nation or corporation can contain its risks alone.

I learned about a fascinating cross-industry forum that brought together an Asian telecom giant, a European automaker, and a Latin American energy company, three industries that rarely find themselves in the same room. Each faced its own version of the AI dilemma: the telecom firm was struggling with data privacy and localization laws; the automaker with accountability in autonomous systems; and the energy company with ensuring inclusion in its workforce analytics. Despite different challenges, they were all wrestling with the same underlying question: *how do you build trust into technology?*

What struck me most, hearing the lessons shared later by one of the participating directors, was how collaboration turned competition into clarity. Instead of comparing who had tighter rules or better AI tools, they co-created a shared governance framework grounded in transparency, fairness, and accountability. That moment illustrated something I've seen repeatedly in boardrooms: when leaders stop debating technology in isolation and start aligning on values, they unlock global trust. AI governance becomes less about control and more about credibility.

Boards can lead such collaborations by

- Joining cross-sector AI ethics alliances.

- Sponsoring regional governance roundtables that include regulators and startups.

- Creating AI oversight committees with external advisors from multiple continents.

The OECD, UNESCO, and NIST AI RMF offer blueprints for such cooperation. Boards that adopt these frameworks don't just comply, they build trust across borders.

I once came across a collaboration between a U.S. industrial firm and a Scandinavian manufacturer that revealed how governance can travel better than technology. Both companies were co-developing an AI system for predictive maintenance, a software capable of flagging equipment failures before they happened. What fascinated me, as I followed the case through an industry consortium I was advising, was how they managed their differences. Instead of arguing over who owned the data or the model, the boards aligned on shared principles: transparency, human oversight, and accountability. Every dataset, every algorithmic adjustment, and every decision point had a clearly identified owner on both sides. The outcome wasn't just safer machinery; it was a model for transnational trust. Two boards, two regulatory environments, one governance language.

I once learned about a Latin American health-tech startup that expanded into Southeast Asia with an AI-driven diagnostics tool designed for faster, low-cost screenings. Early pilots were promising, but the company soon realized its algorithm, trained mostly on Western patient data, was misfiring across Asian populations. Instead of pressing ahead, the founders paused expansion, partnered with regional hospitals, and retrained the model using local datasets with full consent and oversight. The move slowed growth but built deep trust with regulators and investors, who later invited the startup to help shape national AI health standards. It was a reminder I've seen echoed across industries: global adaptability isn't about scaling faster, it's about scaling responsibly, aligning innovation with integrity.

Both stories, one from industry giants and one from a startup with little margin for error, carry the same lesson: AI partnerships, whether global or local, succeed when governance comes first. Alignment on values is what makes innovation sustainable and trust exportable.

Lesson for Boards: Adaptability is the new compliance. The companies that flex intelligently will outlast those that resist context.

Boards and Global Strategy

For directors, the question is not whether to think globally, it's how.

A globally adaptable board doesn't just approve expansion plans; it anticipates friction points such as legal, cultural, reputational.

Boards should challenge management with questions such as how does this strategy translate across cultures? Have we pressure-tested assumptions against local behavior? Do we have the right voices in the room to challenge "home-country bias"?

Insight: Global adaptability begins when boards invite discomfort.

A Framework for Global Adaptability

Boards can institutionalize adaptability through a disciplined framework:

1. **Global Foresight:** Map geopolitical, cultural, and technological trends at every strategic review.

2. **Local Empowerment:** Give regional leaders the autonomy to adapt corporate purpose locally without diluting ethics.

3. **Cross-Cultural Composition:** Appoint directors and advisors from diverse markets—not just diverse backgrounds.

4. **Adaptive Governance:** Build policies that flex with context but preserve core principles of ethics and transparency.

5. **Feedback Loops:** Create global listening posts—customer data, employee sentiment, regulatory feedback—to inform real-time governance.

As a reflection, *when your global strategy fails, is it execution or empathy? Who, in your boardroom, speaks for the customer in Jakarta or Johannesburg? Does your governance model allow variation or enforce uniformity that stifles progress?*

The Next Frontier: A Global Alliance for Responsible AI & The Architecture of Adaptability

As AI becomes the backbone of global economies, the conversation must move from competition to coordination.

Imagine a world where corporations voluntarily align their AI principles through a global AI compact system, anchored in fairness, accountability, and human oversight. Boards that lead this conversation will shape the moral infrastructure of global innovation.

Just as financial standards created stability in the 20th century, AI ethics could define legitimacy in the 21st. The leaders who bridge continents will not only anticipate regulation, they will design it. Their edge will not be speed alone, but credibility.

The leaders of tomorrow will not ask, "Are we a startup or a legacy company?"

They will ask, *"How do we take the best of both and build organizations that can adapt, scale, and endure?"*

Having led across five continents, I've seen that adaptability is not compromise; it is capacity. It is how you translate purpose across languages, borders, and expectations without losing meaning. However, disruption shows up in different ways across continents:

In the U.S., disruption is ambition. In Europe, it is responsibility. In Asia, it is motion. In Latin America and Africa, it is survival and hope.

In a world where disruption moves at different speeds, adaptability is the only constant. It's not a soft trait; it's the system architecture of global resilience. In the end, adaptability is not about surviving change, it's about shaping it. The leaders who master it will not just navigate the global future; they will define it.

In governance, adaptability is not the opposite of consistency, it is consistency evolved. It's the discipline of holding true to core principles while flexing their application across different contexts. Effective boards don't dilute their values to fit diverse realities; they translate them. Adaptability, at its best, is the art of staying grounded in purpose while adjusting the path to fit the terrain.

Closing Reflection: The Responsibility of Leading Across Borders

As you evaluate your own leadership team or board, pause and ask yourself: *Are we building organizations that adapt to the world, or organizations that expect the world to adapt to us?* Global adaptability is not a philosophical trait; it is a practical capability. It requires leaders who read cultural signals as clearly as financial dashboards, who understand that legitimacy in one country may not translate across borders, and who recognize that global influence demands global humility. The boards that thrive over the next decade will treat context as a strategic variable, not a footnote. They will invest intentionally in cultural intelligence, cross-border insight, and the discipline to test assumptions before exporting them.

AI and technology transformation now raise the stakes of this responsibility exponentially. Algorithms do not cross borders as empty vessels, they carry the values, constraints, and design choices of the systems that created them. A model that is compliant in California may be restricted in Berlin. A digital product that scales effortlessly in Seoul may face cultural pushback in São Paulo. Over the years, I've seen companies stumble not because their technology failed technically, but because their leaders failed contextually. The question for every board is now unavoidable: *Are we designing AI that respects local norms, regulations, and expectations or are we allowing technology to collide with culture?* In a world where digital systems travel faster than governance, global adaptability becomes not just a competitive advantage but an ethical safeguard.

When I look back at the organizations that moved fastest—and safest—through disruption, they all shared one trait: they treated adaptability as a discipline, not an accident. They built mechanisms to test assumptions across borders, invited dissent as data, and held firm to shared values even when execution differed by region. They didn't chase a single global playbook; they built a portfolio of local strategies anchored in a common purpose. This chapter is an invitation for you to do the same: to lead with a global mind and local fluency, to turn diversity into direction, and to shape a future where governance travels as confidently as your products.

Chapter 8

The Transformation Playbook for Executives

The Illusion of Transformation

The word transformation has become boardroom wallpaper. Every CEO declares it; every annual report promises it. Yet when you step behind the slogans, what you often find are stalled initiatives, fatigued teams, and leaders chasing momentum that never arrives.

I've sat in those boardrooms, where transformation becomes a calendar item rather than a capability. Where executives describe change in PowerPoint rather than in performance. During my professional experience leading, advising, and observing transformations across industries, I've learned this truth: transformation is not an event, it's a discipline. It doesn't begin with consultants or strategy decks; it begins with leadership architecture—how you align vision, talent, governance, and execution into one continuous loop.

A few years ago, I observed a legacy industrial company navigating a digital crossroads. The leadership team didn't announce a sweeping "transformation initiative" or hire armies of consultants. Instead, they began with small, disciplined shifts: technicians learning data analytics, frontline dashboards replacing manual logs, and weekly briefings that invited curiosity rather than compliance. Within months, the culture started to hum differently. Supervisors discussed customer insights instead of process failures; teams made data-informed choices without waiting for permission. By the time results showed up on quarterly reports, transformation was already visible in daily behavior. No slogans, no reorgs, just quiet alignment between purpose, people, and performance.

If you're a director or senior executive reading this, this chapter will give you a practical playbook, a framework you can immediately apply to diagnose, design, and drive transformation. You'll see how to turn aspiration into measurable progress, how to align competing stakeholders, and how to make change resilient instead of exhausting.

So before diving in, ask yourself: is your organization talking about transformation—or living it? When disruption hits, does your team move with clarity—or with confusion? Are you building a transformation story, or a transformation system?

The Transformation Cycle in Practice

Vision → Talent → Governance → Execution

Transformation is not linear, it's cyclical. The four pillars reinforce each other:

Vision creates direction → Talent drives change → Governance ensures alignment → Execution delivers results → Vision evolves.

This cycle must turn continuously, not episodically. When one pillar weakens, the system slows.

- Without Vision, people lose purpose.
- Without Talent, ideas die in execution.
- Without Governance, chaos spreads.
- Without Execution, transformation remains theater.

I recall analyzing how a European industrial manufacturer transformed its governance approach by hardwiring transformation KPIs directly into its board charter. Each director carried a personal accountability metric, some tied to customer growth or digital maturity, others to carbon reduction or workforce reskilling. Quarterly board meetings no longer discussed transformation as an abstract goal; they reviewed dashboards showing concrete progress. Over time, the conversation shifted from "Are we transforming?" to "*How fast are we learning and scaling?*" That structure turned transformation from a presentation into a performance discipline. Watching this evolution reinforced a lesson I've seen across industries: when boards own part of the transformation scorecard, accountability stops being delegated, it becomes cultural.

Transformation becomes sustainable when it shifts from initiative to identity.

Let's start where all change begins—with vision.

Vision – The Compass of Change

Transformation begins not with a plan, but with a *purpose.*

Every enduring transformation has a clear "why" that connects business necessity to human meaning. When leaders frame transformation as cost-cutting or digital upgrades, employees disengage. When they frame it as a mission, something worth the discomfort, people rally.

I remember working with a manufacturing enterprise that had lost 20 percent of its market share in five years. The board insisted the issue was technology; in truth, it was confusion. Every division had a different definition of success. The CEO finally reset the narrative: "We are not modernizing machines; we are modernizing our purpose: to make sustainability profitable."

That single sentence reframed the company strategy. It linked climate accountability to business growth and gave everyone, from engineers to investors, a shared compass.

During my years operating across five continents, I saw how the same aspiration, growth through innovation, had to be translated into the local language of values and motivation. Transformation only succeeds when people see themselves in the vision.

In Europe, the heartbeat of transformation was sustainability and safety. Teams responded not to profit targets, but to the sense that they were protecting communities and future generations. I remember one industrial operation in Northern Europe that only gained traction on digital transformation once it was framed as a carbon-reduction initiative. The same sensors that optimized energy use also cut emissions, a dual win that aligned innovation with conscience.

In Asia, transformation was a story of opportunity. Employees leaned into change when it promised advancement, new skills, global exposure, and a chance to redefine their careers. In one regional rollout, we discovered that emphasizing "growth of people" rather than "efficiency of systems" turned resistance into energy. The same digital tools that could have been seen as threats became symbols of progress.

In Latin America, purpose lived closer to the heart. Transformation found its rhythm when it was connected to community impact, jobs created, customers served, families supported. When we linked innovation to local pride and social value, engagement soared. A new service platform in Brazil, for instance, wasn't celebrated for its speed or automation, but for enabling thousands of small entrepreneurs to reach new customers.

Vision is universal; resonance is local. The board's challenge is to hold the global purpose steady while letting each market find its own story. Transformation without cultural translation is just strategy on paper. Global vision demands local fluency.

Creating a strong vision starts with clarity of purpose and emotional resonance. It's not a slogan crafted in a retreat, it's a conviction that connects ambition to meaning. The most effective leaders build vision from three anchors: truth, context, and aspiration. Truth grounds the vision in reality, what the organization truly stands for and where it must improve. Context aligns that truth to global forces like technology, regulation, and culture. Aspiration stretches beyond comfort zones, offering employees and stakeholders a story they want to belong to. In the boardroom, this means framing vision as both a compass and a contract, clear enough to guide decisions, yet flexible enough to evolve as markets shift.

Ask yourself: *Can every person in your organization explain why transformation matters now? Does your vision connect to both global trends (AI, digitalization, sustainability) and local realities (culture, regulation, behavior)? When you speak about transformation, do people feel urgency or fatigue?*

A strong vision does not just describe a destination; it creates alignment in uncertainty.

Talent – The Real Engine of Change

Strategy may set the direction, but people carry the load.

No transformation succeeds without the right talent architecture. Yet too many boards spend months refining strategy slides while neglecting the human infrastructure that makes them real. Transformation is not written, it is lived.

Years ago, I advised a telecom that announced a "digital reinvention." Millions were budgeted for cloud migration and AI systems. But inside the organization, fear spread faster than enthusiasm. Engineers worried about redundancy; managers hoarded information to protect turf. The turning point came not from technology but from training. The company launched an enterprise-wide reskilling program, treating learning as a benefit, not a burden. Within a year, 70 percent of employees had completed digital-skills certifications, productivity rose by 20 percent, and internal mobility doubled. Transformation stopped being something done to people; it became something done with them.

Contrast that with a competitor that cut staff and outsourced innovation. Costs dropped briefly—then creativity evaporated. When 5G arrived, they had no internal champions left to lead adoption. Talent is transformation's multiplier. The formula is simple:

Vision × Talent = Velocity.

Implementing the Vision × Talent approach starts by treating alignment as a daily discipline, not a quarterly reminder. Begin with the vision, make it visible, measurable, and human. Every leader should be able to explain in one sentence how their team's work advances that vision. Then connect the right talent to the right moments of transformation. This means mapping critical capabilities, digital, operational, and cultural and ensuring each has an accountable leader empowered to act. Boards can reinforce this by linking transformation milestones to people metrics: retention of top performers, speed of decision-making, and employee engagement around purpose.

I recall a company that I observed and which used "vision cascades", brief, focused dialogues where every manager linked their team goals directly to strategic outcomes. Within months, communication gaps closed, decision speed doubled, and innovation proposals surged. The formula proved true: when vision and talent move together, transformation accelerates not because of slogans, but because everyone understands where they're going and feels equipped to get there.

Your role on the Board of Directors is to ensure that velocity is sustainable. That means:

- Empowering change agents at every level—those who see opportunity where others see risk.

- Blending legacy expertise with entrepreneurial hires who challenge assumptions.

- Investing in learning velocity—the rate at which teams can absorb and apply new skills.

- Developing the right transformation metrics — beyond financials, boards must track capability and cultural progress. For example, measure the number of ideas tested per quarter, decision-cycle time, employee readiness scores, and customer experience impact.

These indicators reveal whether transformation is taking root or stalling beneath the surface. What gets measured gets managed and what gets measured wisely gets accelerated.

So, *who in your organization is shaping the future, and who is anchoring it? Are your reward systems built for stability or for learning? Does your transformation budget allocate more to technology than to talent? If so, invert it. Can your frontline teams clearly see how their work connects to your company's transformation story or are they still guessing what the vision really means? If you walked into a project meeting tomorrow, would people speak in the language of alignment or activity?*

The difference defines velocity. The Vision × Talent approach is not about adding new programs; it's about tightening the connection between purpose and people until execution becomes instinctive. When that happens, transformation no longer depends on top-down mandates, it becomes a shared movement that propels the entire organization forward.

Governance – Guardrails That Enable Speed

Governance often gets blamed for slowing transformation. But when designed right, it's not a brake, it's the steering wheel. True transformation governance balances freedom to innovate with discipline to stay aligned. Without it, organizations either drift in chaos or calcify in control.

I learned this during a post-merger integration where two cultures collided: one agile and entrepreneurial, the other process-driven and hierarchical. Early meetings were chaos, everyone talked, no one decided. We redesigned governance around three principles:

1. Clear decision rights—who decides what, by when.

2. Transparent metrics—visible dashboards that tracked both progress and risk.

3. Board cadence—quarterly transformation reviews focused on learning, not blame.

Within six months, projects that had languished for a year began closing in weeks.

I worked with a multinational manufacturing company that took this further, creating a "Transformation Dashboard" for its board, a one-page visual of KPIs, milestones, and risks. Instead of waiting for annual reviews, directors could see red flags in real time. Transformation moved from anecdote to evidence.

Transformation governance, at its core, demands sharper questions and faster answers. You should be asking: are our transformation decisions being made fast enough to stay relevant in a shifting market, or are we trapped in analysis while competitors act? Are emerging risks, cultural resistance, digital fatigue, or execution drift, surfacing early enough for intervention, or only after they've derailed progress? And are accountability lines for transformation outcomes crystal clear, or buried under overlapping committees and vague ownership? Transformation dies not from lack of ambition, but from unclear governance. If you can't pinpoint who decides, who monitors, and who owns results, then your transformation isn't being led, it's being managed by inertia.

Startups already live this way. They run lean governance with heavy accountability. Corporations can do the same by designing light processes, hard metrics.

To implement transformation governance with guardrails that enable speed, boards must replace bureaucratic checkpoints with decision architecture — structures that guide, not hinder, momentum.

- Start by defining who decides what at each level: strategic pivots belong to the board, resource reallocations to executives, and operational experiments to empowered teams.

- Establish a clear "two-way visibility" system — short, focused transformation dashboards that show real-time progress, risk signals, and course corrections without endless reports.

- Use tiered governance rhythms: quarterly reviews for strategic alignment, monthly pulse checks for risk and talent indicators, and weekly execution sprints within teams.

- Build lightweight escalation rules so issues rise fast but decisions don't bottleneck.

- Create an explicit "green zone" — areas where innovation teams can move without prior approval — and a "red zone" which ethical, financial, or reputational risk triggers immediate oversight. Transformation governance, when done right, acts like a Formula One pit crew: tight guardrails, rapid adjustments, and a shared mission to keep the car on the track and ahead of the race.

Remember: Speed without control is chaos. Control without speed is stagnation. Governance is where the two meet.

Execution – Turning Vision into Momentum

Most transformations die in execution not because leaders lack vision, but because they lose focus. Execution is where clarity meets consistency.

The challenge isn't ambition; it's discipline. I once observed a global consumer company that launched a bold digital campaign. The vision was strong, but initiatives multiplied uncontrollably, 120 projects, 50 KPIs, no sequence. Momentum dissolved.

A new COO reset the model in a way that every transformation initiative had to produce a measurable customer or employee outcome within 90 days. Anything longer required board justification. That constraint sparked creativity. Teams broke massive goals into micro-wins, new digital onboarding in one region, predictive analytics for supply in another. Within a year, digital revenue grew almost 30 percent.

Execution demands structure without suffocation:

- Short cycles: 90-day sprints for quick learning.
- Visible wins: Celebrate early adopters.
- Customer anchor: If it doesn't improve experience, question its relevance.

Execution is where transformation moves from strategy decks to daily discipline. I recall when a large national franchisor in the quick-service restaurant industry transformed its fragmented operations by treating governance as collaboration, not control. Rather than imposing uniform systems, leadership formed a joint taskforce with franchisees to co-design a digital operations platform, shared performance dashboards, and clear accountability metrics. The result: faster service, double-digit cost savings, and a measurable rise in customer satisfaction. The transformation worked because it blended structure with trust, proving that even in fast-moving networks, governance done right can accelerate innovation instead of slowing it.

Driving execution at this level requires relentless clarity and cadence. Set measurable outcomes that connect strategy to behavior, service time, cost-to-serve, or engagement scores. Hold brief, high-frequency reviews instead of long quarterly postmortems. Empower local teams to act within defined parameters and escalate only when thresholds are breached. Make data visible across the organization so decisions travel as fast as information. And most importantly, ensure the board remains engaged in outcomes, not just oversight, tracking progress, removing bottlenecks, and celebrating visible wins. Execution is not about doing more; it's about doing what matters most, faster, and with shared accountability.

What made the transformation work wasn't just the technology, it was trust built through structured collaboration, clear governance, and visible accountability. Execution, at scale, is not about control; it's about coordination.

In your boardroom, *does your transformation roadmap translate into visible progress every quarter or does it linger in presentations no one revisits? Are you measuring outcomes that people can feel customer satisfaction, speed, engagement or just internal outputs and activity? How many of your "strategic priorities" have actually reached the customer?* Sustainable execution is not about managing more projects; it's about creating visible traction. The most effective leaders make transformation tangible, tracking what changes in the field, not just what's discussed in the meeting. That's how accountability moves from paper to performance.

Aligning Stakeholders in Times of Disruption

Transformation succeeds when everyone sees themselves in it.

Disruption tests stakeholder alignment more than strategy. Shareholders demand returns; employees crave stability; customers expect consistency; regulators require compliance. The executive's task is not to silence these tensions but to synchronize them.

A valuable tool I've seen boards use during disruption is the Stakeholder Heat Map, a living radar system that highlights alignment and friction before they become crises. The map evaluates each stakeholder group across two dimensions: alignment (support for the company's transformation) and influence (their power to accelerate or obstruct). Core groups typically include investors, employees, customers, regulators, supply-chain partners, and community stakeholders. Building the map requires disciplined listening and evidence-based assessment, using engagement metrics, surveys, analyst reports, sentiment analysis, and qualitative feedback from frontline leaders.

Once drafted, the map is color-coded, green for alignment, yellow for emerging tension, red for resistance. The real value comes when the board reviews it quarterly, tracking shifts in sentiment: investor confidence trending up or down, employee engagement slipping, customer loyalty softening, or regulatory posture tightening. A yellow or red square triggers inquiry rather than defensiveness. It prompts targeted outreach, town halls, investor check-ins, customer listening sessions, to understand what is changing and why.

For you as a leader, the Stakeholder Heat Map forces a habit of anticipation rather than reaction. It helps you test assumptions, see the full system of relationships around your transformation, and ask sharper questions: Where are we losing trust? Where are we overestimating alignment? How do we prevent concern from becoming a public issue? Used consistently, the map becomes a strategic early-warning system, one of the simplest ways to ensure alignment, build credibility, and maintain momentum in times of disruption.

As an example, during a digital transformation review at an anonymized industrial company, the board noticed a sudden shift: employee engagement had moved from green to yellow, driven by concerns about automation and job redesign. At the same time, regulators shifted from yellow to red after new AI guidelines were introduced. Investors remained green but requested clearer KPIs. The board used the heat map to guide next steps: the CEO hosted employee listening sessions, the Chief Compliance Officer met with regulators to clarify expectations, and the board requested a revised communication plan tied to measurable milestones. Within one quarter, employee sentiment returned to green and regulatory concerns were reduced to yellow.

I advised an energy company that used this method during its pivot to renewables. Instead of hiding the trade-offs, it hosted open sessions with unions, environmental NGOs, and local communities. The process slowed rollout but strengthened legitimacy. The CEO later said, "We traded speed for sustainability and gained both." Transformation requires not just alignment around *what* to change, but empathy for *who* is changing with you.

As a board member, *have you mapped your stakeholders by both power and passion? How are you communicating trade-offs transparently? When disruption hits, who hears from you first, the investors or the employees?*

Stakeholder alignment isn't a PR exercise. It's the operating system of trust.

Measuring Transformation Progress

You can't govern what you can't measure, and you can't measure transformation with yesterday's metrics. Boards traditionally rely on lagging indicators: revenue, margins, ROI. Transformation demands *leading* indicators that capture adaptation, learning, and cultural energy.

As a board member, I would like to share a few I've seen boards adopt successfully:

- Execution Rate – % of strategic initiatives completed on time and within budget.
- Adoption Rate – % of employees actively using or applying new tools, processes, or systems introduced by transformation.
- Learning Progress – Average number of completed training or upskilling hours per employee per quarter.
- Trust & Engagement Score – Derived from short quarterly surveys measuring trust in leadership, clarity of communication, and confidence in company direction.
- Customer Satisfaction – Measures whether transformation improves the customer experience.
- Revenue or Efficiency Impact – Tracks measurable financial outcomes (e.g., % improvement in productivity, margin, or cost reduction) tied directly to transformation projects.

- Stakeholder Confidence Index – Simple pulse check (1–5 scale) from investors, employees, and partners about the organization's transformation momentum and direction.

Boards should review transformation dashboards quarterly, treating misses as learning, not failure. Transparency transforms skepticism into credibility.

Metrics only matter when they provoke the right conversations. The most effective leaders don't just track numbers, they use them to listen, learn, and lead better. So, ask yourself: *Are your transformation metrics telling a story of progress or of activity without impact? Do they measure what truly changes for your customers, employees, and stakeholders, or just what gets reported? When was the last time your board reviewed not just the pace of transformation, but the confidence behind it? What would your Transformation Dashboard show if published publicly tomorrow? Which metrics reflect learning and trust, not just output?*

Entrepreneurial Parallels

In entrepreneurship, transformation is not optional, it's survival.

During the pandemic, one of our consumer-service ventures faced shutdowns overnight. There was no guidance, no committees; we had to improvise. Within weeks, teams redesigned customer experiences for safety, launched online bookings, and converted local marketing into community engagement. Those actions didn't just save revenue, they deepened trust.

What struck me later was how similar that experience was to the transformation challenges in global corporations. The only difference was scale and pace. Startups pivot by instinct; corporates pivot by governance. The best systems combine both: entrepreneurial urgency with institutional discipline.

A mid-size logistics startup I followed during that same period thrived because it operationalized experimentation. Every week was a mini-review: what worked, what failed, what to test next. That cadence is something large organizations can emulate, smaller experiments, faster feedback, governed learning.

So, *how can your board create safe spaces for experimentation without losing oversight? Do your governance systems reward learning or only punish failure?*

The Executive Transformation Mindset

The hardest part of transformation is not technology, it's psychology.

Executives must model vulnerability before demanding adaptability. The leaders who succeed in transformation are those willing to unlearn. They shift from "expert" to "experimenter," from controlling decisions to empowering curiosity.

I recall a CEO who began his town halls with this line: "We are in year one of becoming beginners again." That humility galvanized trust. His team stopped pretending to have all the answers and started collaborating across silos. Transformation requires executives to lead by example:

- Curiosity over certainty.
- Transparency over perfection.
- Consistency over charisma.

Boards can encourage this by integrating learning goals into executive evaluations and scheduling "governance retrospectives" where directors review not just performance, but adaptability.

In your company or the board that you serve, when was the last time your leadership team admitted, "We don't know, let's test"? Do your board meetings celebrate progress or only perfection?

Closing Reflection – From Change Management to Change Mastery

Transformation isn't about chasing every trend. It's about mastering renewal as a habit.

The most successful organizations treat transformation as muscle memory—trained, tested, and strengthened continuously. They embed learning loops, invest in resilience, and build governance systems that keep purpose and progress aligned.

For you as a leader, the invitation is clear:

- Make transformation visible, measurable, and human.
- Govern it as a system, not a slogan.
- Treat disruption not as an interruption, but as your competitive edge.

Because in the end, transformation is not a race, it's a rhythm. The rhythm of vision made clear, talent empowered, governance disciplined, and execution relentless.

When that rhythm becomes instinct, disruption ceases to threaten and it becomes the pulse of progress.

If your organization faced another global shock tomorrow, would you improvise or be ready? What part of your playbook still lives in slides and what part already beats in behavior?

Transformation is not about being the fastest to change; it's about being the most deliberate in how you lead it. And the leaders who master that discipline won't just navigate the future, they'll define it.

Chapter 9

The Startup Governance Playbook

A few years ago, I sat in on a startup board meeting that lasted barely forty minutes, but those forty minutes revealed everything about the DNA of young companies. The founder spoke with conviction, investors pushed for clarity, and the board chair scribbled notes as the team debated whether to pivot or persevere. There were no long slide decks, no polished speeches, just urgency, tension, and vision colliding in real time. It was messy, fast, and deeply human. That's the reality of startup governance: it's not about formalities; it's about alignment under pressure.

Every startup begins with a spark, a founder's conviction that speed will outpace scale. But somewhere between the first investor check and the first regulatory letter, that spark meets friction. Board meetings multiply. Advisors debate strategy. Investors ask for reports. Suddenly, the company that once thrived on freedom begins to wrestle with formality.

That's where most founders panic. They equate *governance* with *bureaucracy*, assuming that rules will kill innovation. But governance, done right, doesn't slow companies down, it makes speed sustainable. It's not about control; it's about clarity.

In the past decade advising and observing early-stage ventures, I've seen both sides: startups that collapsed under chaos because they had no structure, and others that scaled successfully because they treated governance as part of their operating system from day one.

If you're a founder, investor, or startup board member, this chapter is for you. It will help you understand:

- How governance maturity evolves through seed, growth, and scale stages.
- What healthy founder-board dynamics look like (and how they go wrong).
- When and how to add structure without killing agility.
- The frameworks, tools, and mindsets that turn governance into a growth accelerator.

So, before we dive in, ask yourself: *Is your board a partner or a referee? Do your investors challenge strategy or only react to results? And most importantly: are you building a company that can govern itself when you're not in the room?*

Let's unpack how governance evolves and why founders who master it never outgrow it.

The Three Phases of Startup Governance

Governance in startups isn't binary; it's a maturity curve. The discipline that feels like "overkill" in year one becomes survival insurance by year five. Here's how it typically evolves:

Phase 1: Seed Stage – Trust and Advisory

At the seed stage, governance is built on people, not processes. Founders rely on trust more than bylaws. Advisory boards, often composed of friends, mentors, and early investors serve as sounding boards, not watchdogs.

A founder I mentored once described his early board meetings as "therapy sessions with a spreadsheet." Cash flow dominated every conversation: burn rate, runway, and unit economics. The goal wasn't compliance; it was survival.

But even in this informality, structure matters. A simple monthly financial review, a cap table check, and transparent investor updates can make or break credibility. Early discipline signals maturity.

One early marketplace venture I observed raised seed funding quickly but had no structured board. When co-founders disagreed on pricing and expansion, investors had no visibility and confidence eroded. Within months, new capital dried up. A competitor, with nearly identical technology but a basic advisory board and monthly reporting cadence, kept investor trust and secured a Series A within six months.

Governance is not about formality; it's about credibility. At the seed stage, governance is the difference between investors believing your vision or believing you'll vanish. In these early moments, investors don't just evaluate your product or market, they evaluate you. They watch how you handle uncertainty, how you make decisions under pressure, and how transparent you are about what you don't yet know. For most startups, governance starts long before the first board meeting; it begins in every conversation where a founder earns or loses investor trust.

So, *are your advisors empowered to challenge you or just to cheer you on? Do you track decisions or rely on memory? How often do your investors hear from you between funding rounds? Are you coachable and agile to quickly adapt to the market requirements?*

Seed-stage governance builds the habit of accountability before it becomes an obligation.

Phase 2: Growth Stage – Structure and Alignment

Growth exposes cracks that seed-stage enthusiasm can't fix. Decision-making becomes complex, reporting demands rise, and the first signs of governance fatigue appear.

This is where startups must evolve from trust-based leadership to system-based leadership. Formal fiduciary boards emerge. Decision rights are documented. Founder control begins to share space with investor oversight.

It's also where the founder-board relationship can turn from partnership to tension.

I recall learning from an investor-director who joined a scaling fintech company at this exact stage. The founder resisted adding independent directors, arguing that "they'd slow us down." Within a year, a compliance failure triggered regulatory scrutiny, and the absence of oversight nearly cost them their license. The same founder later admitted, "The board didn't slow us down, it saved us."

As you may recall, Uber's early governance model concentrated control in the founder's hands. For years, that worked until culture and compliance issues went unchecked. It took board intervention, independent directors, and governance reform to stabilize the company.

Governance isn't about founders losing control; it's about learning to share it responsibly. As a company evolves, so must its leadership style. The early instinct to do everything alone, the late-night decisions, the all-hands improvisation must give way to structured delegation and specialized expertise. This is the stage where a founder begins to transform into a true CEO: hiring functional leaders, establishing clear processes, and creating systems that outlive individual effort. Governance, at this point, becomes the operating rhythm that allows the organization to scale without chaos. The best founders don't see it as surrendering control, they see it as multiplying their capacity through trust, discipline, and well-designed accountability. And in some cases, the seed and growth phases overlap; structure and agility must coexist as the company experiments, matures, and learns to professionalize without losing its entrepreneurial spirit.

At the growth stage:

- Formal boards replace informal advisors.
- Fiduciary duties (care, loyalty, compliance) become real.
- Board diversity (skill, geography, gender) improves decision quality.
- Performance dashboards replace gut feel.

So, ask yourself: *Does your board have the right skills or just familiar faces? Are you spending more time justifying the past quarter or shaping the next one? Have you defined when decisions need board approval and when they don't?*

Clarity here is not red tape, it's your growth insurance policy.

Phase 3: Scale Stage – Institutionalization and Resilience

By the time startups enter scale mode, they resemble mid-sized enterprises but often with governance systems still built for speed, not stability.

This stage demands institutionalized discipline: audit committees, risk oversight, compensation alignment, ESG frameworks, and global compliance systems. Yet it must remain lean. Over governance kills entrepreneurship as surely as under-governance kills trust.

A rapidly expanding payments company learned this balance the hard way. As it scaled across five continents, regulatory complexity grew faster than revenue. Each new market brought its own licensing rules, data-privacy requirements, and financial-crime frameworks. Initially, the company tried to manage everything from headquarters with one board, one compliance team, one process. Within a year, it drowned in delays and local missteps.

Rather than adding bureaucracy, leadership designed a "two-speed governance model." The global board focused on macro priorities such as enterprise risk, capital allocation, cybersecurity, and strategic partnerships, while regional advisory boards were empowered to move fast on market-specific issues such as product localization, customer onboarding, and regulatory relations. Each region submitted a quarterly "trust and compliance pulse" report: key risks, local regulatory changes, and customer-impact metrics.

The result was alignment without gridlock. The global board could see risks in real time without second-guessing local decisions, and regional teams felt ownership rather than oversight. In less than two years, the company's cross-border transaction volume tripled while regulatory citations dropped by half. The model became a reference point for how governance can scale without suffocating innovation. In summary, faster decisions, compliant growth, and zero major regulatory incidents in four years.

The best time to institutionalize governance is *before* you need it.

So, *do your committees reflect today's risks or yesterday's structure? Can your governance scale globally without adding friction? If your board meeting minutes were published tomorrow, would they build confidence or concern?*

At scale, governance becomes culture. It's how organizations earn the right to keep growing.

The Founder–Board Relationship: From Control to Collaboration

One of the most defining (and delicate) dynamics in startup life is between the founder and the board. Done right, it's a partnership that compounds wisdom. Done wrong, it becomes a cold war.

The best boards operate like co-pilots, not traffic police. They push, challenge, and support without hijacking the flight path. The worst ones either disengage entirely or oversteer from the backseat.

A founder once told me, "I don't need a board; I need believers." I understood the sentiment but belief without accountability is not governance; it's groupthink. Here's the reality: founders bring vision; boards bring perspective. When those align, governance becomes innovation's ally.

Airbnb's early board reflected this balance. Its investors acted as mentors, helping the founders navigate regulatory crises and trust challenges without dictating daily operations. That blend of empathy and oversight helped Airbnb professionalize its systems without losing its community spirit.

Contrast that with startups that resist external input. I've seen brilliant founders lose companies they built because they refused to build trust with their boards. Governance failure often begins with ego, not ethics.

So, *do your board meetings feel like performance reviews or strategy sessions? Are dissenting voices valued or avoided? Is your board composition built for your next stage—or your last round? Do you listen to your board?*

As one seasoned director once said to me, "The goal isn't to control the founder—it's to protect the mission."

Advisory Boards vs. Fiduciary Boards

In early stages, startups often mix these up and pay the price later.

Advisory boards are informal. They guide, mentor, and open doors but they carry no legal responsibility. Their power lies in wisdom, not votes. Fiduciary boards, on the other hand, hold legal accountability for the company's actions. They represent shareholders, enforce compliance, and can hire or fire CEOs.

Many founders make the mistake of creating "hybrid boards" that do neither well. Advisors who expect influence but avoid liability, and directors who lack clarity about authority.

Here's a simple way to distinguish:

- If you want feedback, create an advisory board.
- If you need oversight, create a fiduciary board.

As companies grow, both can coexist, but their boundaries must be explicit.

I once mentored a founder who resisted formalizing her board. "Everyone's already giving advice," she said, half-joking but half-true. Her startup had grown fast on energy and intuition with friends, early investors, and mentors all weighing in when needed. But when a data privacy issue emerged after a customer complaint, that informal network vanished into ambiguity. Who was responsible? Who had authority to act? Advice without accountability suddenly had no power. Within a week, she made the call to formalize governance: appointing two independent directors, one legal expert who understood compliance frameworks and one operator with experience scaling customer data systems. Their presence immediately changed the tone of decision-making. Meetings became sharper, risk reviews were structured, and investor confidence rose. Within six months, the company had rebuilt trust, secured a new funding round, and turned what once felt like "bureaucracy" into a strategic advantage.

Governance clarity isn't bureaucracy, it's risk insurance.

Right-Sized Governance: The Framework

Startups don't need corporate governance, they need right-sized governance. Too much structure, and you smother the very agility that makes early-stage companies innovative. Too little, and you drift into the kind of chaos that destroys trust with investors, customers, and employees. The real discipline is learning how to calibrate governance to the stage of the company tightening where stakes rise, loosening where creativity matters, and always protecting the founder's ability to execute with speed. Right-sized governance means giving the team enough freedom to build, enough accountability to stay grounded, and enough visibility so investors know the company is learning, not guessing. It is the craft of designing oversight that grows with the company rather than constraining it.

Right-Sized Governance Framework

Stage	Structure	Key Focus	Governance Role
Seed	Advisory Board	Cash discipline, founder mentorship	Credibility
Growth	Formal Board	Accountability, investor trust	Alignment
Scale	Committees, Independent Directors	Sustainability, risk oversight	Legitimacy

Think of this not as a checklist, but as a lens through which leadership decisions are made. Governance grows with complexity, not vanity. Governance maturity isn't a switch you flip; it's a system you build over time. The key is right-sizing adding the right structure at the right stage.

At the seed stage, governance is about credibility, not control. Founders should start with an advisory board, not a formal one including three to five trusted voices who bring domain expertise, legal or financial literacy, and access to early networks. The key is regular cadence: monthly or biweekly check-ins with a shared, concise agenda (cash runway, key risks, hiring pipeline, product milestones). Founders can reinforce trust by documenting decisions in short "board notes," even when no board yet exists. This simple discipline signals accountability to investors and helps the founder think like a fiduciary before one is required.

During the growth stage, as funding rounds grow and headcount expands, governance must evolve from informal advice to structured oversight. This is where the fiduciary board emerges typically three to five members, including at least one independent director. Founders should define clear decision rights: what management owns, what requires board approval, and what can be delegated to committees. A light governance rhythm helps: quarterly formal meetings complemented by monthly touchpoints. This is also the time to introduce core policies, financial controls, conflict-of-interest declarations, and early audit readiness. The goal is not to slow down decisions but to give them clarity. A well-run growth-stage board acts as a multiplier, aligning investors, founders, and leadership around shared metrics and accountability.

At scale, the company begins to look more like an enterprise but must guard against corporate rigidity. Governance now includes specialized committees, audit, risk, and compensation, but their design should remain lean. A transformation dashboard at the board level keeps visibility high: key KPIs on performance, culture, customer satisfaction, and risk exposure. Directors should undergo annual board-effectiveness reviews, and the company should formalize succession planning for both executive and board roles. Crucially, independence becomes a strength: diverse, global voices provide external perspective and credibility with regulators, investors, and customers.

In practice, these stages rarely progress in perfect sequence. A fast-scaling startup may need growth-level structure before closing a Series A. A late-stage startup expanding globally may add risk committees even before IPO. What matters is proportionality matching governance depth to the company's complexity, not its valuation. The smartest founders build hybrid systems: they keep advisory boards for innovation and customer insights while the fiduciary board manages accountability and risk. This layered approach preserves agility while embedding the discipline needed for sustainable scale.

Ultimately, right-sized governance is less about formality and more about readiness. It ensures founders stay ahead of complexity rather than reacting to it, transforming governance from a burden into a strategic advantage.

Periodically audit your board by asking key questions such as does our structure fit our current risk profile? Are our meetings focused on learning or reporting? Are we spending time on what drives enterprise value or what's easy to measure? Which skills and expertise do we need to add to the board?

Right-sized governance is what keeps founders free to innovate while keeping investors confident enough to fund the journey.

Lessons from Entrepreneurship: Governance as Trust

When I shifted from global corporations to entrepreneurial ventures, I learned that governance feels different at every scale, but it means the same thing everywhere: trust.

At one technology venture I advised, governance came through founder councils. These weren't bureaucratic committees; they were fast-moving, cross-functional sessions, where each week, product, finance, and operations leads aligned decisions. Each meeting ended with one rule: every idea needed an owner, a metric, and a timeline. It wasn't about control; it was about clarity. The discipline kept teams focused and investors informed. Within a year, what began as an informal startup rhythm matured into a scalable governance model, one that balanced innovation with accountability.

When governance creates clarity on equity, communication and performance, it builds psychological safety for teams and credibility for investors.

Founders often underestimate how much investors value governance. A Series A term sheet may come from believing in you and your product, but a Series C investment comes from believing in your systems.

Governance, at its best, institutionalizes trust faster than risk can erode it. So, *how transparent are your financials to investors and employees? When decisions go wrong, do you blame or learn? Does your board measure trust or just targets?*

Building Scale-Ready Boards

As startups scale, governance maturity must scale too. Many boards fail because they never evolve their composition. By the time a startup enters its scale phase, the conversation in the boardroom shifts from *"Can we grow?"* to *"Can we grow responsibly and globally?"* Scale-ready boards look different because they think differently. They don't just review metrics; they anticipate inflection points. They balance entrepreneurial instinct with institutional discipline.

1. Diversity of Expertise – Seeing Around Corners
Scale introduces complexity, financial, technological, regulatory, and cultural. Boards that thrive at this stage intentionally blend expertise. A director with cybersecurity experience can spot risks in AI or data strategy long before they become headlines. A director from a consumer background can challenge assumptions about customer experience in new markets. One fintech I followed intentionally recruited a former regulator and a behavioral scientist to its board as it prepared to enter Europe. The result wasn't slower decisions; it was smarter foresight. Diversity of expertise isn't about optics; it's about resilience.

2. Operator Experience – From Theory to Practice
At scale, strategy slides are easy; execution under pressure isn't. Boards need directors who have lived through expansion, restructuring, or transformation, not just those who have financed it. Operators understand what it means to hire 1,000 people in a year, navigate supply chain shocks, or sustain culture across time zones. I've seen the difference first-hand: one fast-scaling energy-tech company brought in a director who had previously led operations across three continents. His questions changed the tone of board meetings from "Can we?" to "Have we tested this under pressure?" That single addition transformed optimism into operational readiness.

3. Cultural Intelligence – Global Mindset, Local Sensitivity
Scaling isn't just adding markets; it's entering new social contracts. Cultural intelligence gives the board the ability to interpret how values, norms, and regulations shape business outcomes. A safety campaign that motivates teams in Houston might confuse those in Jakarta. A compliance policy that works in Europe may fail in Latin America if it doesn't acknowledge local dynamics. I remember a global board that included directors from four continents; their debates were lively, but their decisions were grounded in reality. That cross-cultural tension was a strength. It kept the company from assuming what worked "at home" would work everywhere.

A few years ago, a SaaS startup I observed replaced one investor seat with an independent director, an experienced CFO from a public tech company. That shift reframed the board's role from transactional oversight to strategic stewardship. As a result, board discussions moved from capital structure debates to strategic growth planning. Within 18 months, revenue tripled, and governance maturity became a selling point in its Series D round.

Scale-ready boards treat governance not as a reporting burden but as a strategic asset. They view board composition as a living portfolio: technology fluency, operational scars, and cultural range evolve as the company grows. The best boards schedule annual "skills audits" to identify gaps aligned with future strategy. If the company is moving into AI, sustainability, or emerging markets, the board evolves in parallel.

At scale, the question isn't who controls the momentum, it's who enables it. The board's real job is to make sure the company can grow with discipline, adapt with confidence, and pursue bold ambitions without compromising its values. A scale-ready board doesn't just oversee; it expands the organization's capacity to go further, faster, and safer.

Founder Resilience and Board Evolution

The founder's journey often mirrors the company's governance maturity. At first, the founder *is* the board and every decision runs through one person. Over time, survival depends on learning to delegate, debate, and share accountability.

A founder who refuses governance is like a pilot who refuses instrument trusting instinct until the weather turns.

The most self-aware founders I've known viewed governance as leadership development. They surrounded themselves with directors who challenged assumptions, not personalities. As one said to me, "I don't need my board to agree with me; I need them to make me sharper."

So, *have you designed your board to make you better or to make you comfortable? Do your directors know your blind spots and are they empowered to call them out? Is your governance evolving faster than your business?*

Founders who mature their governance grow faster, raise smarter, and fail safer.

Closing Reflection – Governance as the Growth Multiplier

At its core, startup governance is not about control, it's about clarity. The founders who embrace governance early build companies that scale without losing soul. They understand that speed without structure burns out, and structure without speed stagnates.

In a world where investors demand transparency, regulators demand accountability, and employees demand trust, governance becomes your greatest differentiator.

So, *ask yourself as you close this chapter, does your startup have the governance it deserves or just the governance it inherited? If tomorrow brought a crisis, funding shortfall, compliance issue, reputational risk, would your board be ready to lead, or would it freeze? And most importantly, are you building a company that will outlast your energy and your ownership?*

Because governance, when done right, doesn't just protect growth, it propels it. It turns founders into leaders, investors into partners, and startups into institutions.

That is the true playbook for sustainable success.

Chapter 10

The Board of the Future

There is a silent transformation of the boardroom. Imagine walking into a boardroom a decade from now. The agenda looks familiar, financials, risk, strategy, but the conversation is not. A director questions the bias in an AI model used for loan approvals. Another director challenges whether the company's climate disclosures meet new global standards. A third one points out that a viral social post from an employee in Jakarta could trigger a supply-chain backlash in Europe overnight. The room feels different, not quieter, but sharper. It's not about authority anymore; it's about awareness.

That is the board of the future. And parts of that future are already here.

Over the last several years, sitting in boardrooms across industries and geographies, I've seen a clear divide emerge. There are boards that have already begun to transform—learning, experimenting, and reshaping how they govern technology, talent, and trust. There are boards that know change is coming and are actively trying to catch up. And there are boards still in "wait and see" mode, confident that experience and past success will buy them more time. History suggests otherwise.

For much of the last century, boards were built for oversight: steady hands, quarterly reviews, predictable routines. That model worked in a world where change was incremental. But in the 21st century, stability is the exception. Markets move faster than governance cycles. Technology scales decisions instantly.

Reputation can erode globally in hours. The future now demands boards that act not only as overseers, but as stewards of trust, technology, and long-term value.

We've seen what happens when boards and companies fail to adjust. BlackBerry once dominated secure mobile communications, trusted by governments and enterprises worldwide. The technology shifts were visible. The signals were clear, but the board and leadership clung to legacy assumptions about customers, platforms, and control. By the time governance caught up to innovation, the market had already moved on. Kodak tells a similar story, not of ignorance, but of hesitation. Technology existed, insight existed and what failed was the willingness to govern transformation decisively. These were not product failures; they were governance failures.

This is the uncomfortable truth: if boards do not transform how they think, learn, and govern, some companies simply will not exist ten years from now. Not because they lacked talent or capital but because governance lagged reality.

This chapter explores how boardrooms must evolve: from compliance to curiosity, from control to stewardship, and from closed networks to global ecosystems of learning. You'll see how the role of the director is shifting and why directors who do not adapt risk becoming irrelevant to the very organizations they are meant to protect.

You'll learn what competencies tomorrow's directors must master—technology fluency, cultural intelligence, ethical agility, and continuous learning—and how boards can redesign themselves to remain legitimate and effective in an age where disruption is constant and trust must be earned repeatedly.

As you read, ask yourself: *Which type of board are you on today, the one already evolving, the one learning under pressure, or the one still waiting? Does your board operate as a quarterly review committee or as a strategic nerve center? When technology or ethics enters the conversation, does the room lean in or tune out? And if your organization were judged tomorrow on the transparency, fairness, and foresight of its decisions, would your board be ready or exposed?*

Directors Competencies to Master

In an era of accelerating complexity, technological disruption, and heightened stakeholder expectations, board effectiveness is no longer defined by experience alone. Directors must deliberately build a modern set of competencies that enable them to govern not just for control, but for resilience, trust, and long-term value creation. The following competencies represent a practical blueprint for boards directors seeking to remain relevant, credible, and impactful in the years ahead.

Let's start with stewardship. The traditional role of the board was to watch over management. The future role is to walk alongside it. Oversight ensures compliance; stewardship ensures coherence between purpose, performance, and public trust.

The board of the future must serve as the conscience of the corporation. It asks whether innovation respects human values, whether sustainability goals align with profit motives, and whether leadership decisions earn, not demand, public trust.

One global food manufacturer I once observed during a governance review made this shift with striking clarity. When its supply chain came under scrutiny for environmental impact, the board didn't just demand reports, it visited field operations, met with community leaders, and reframed the company's sustainability strategy around shared value. That single act reshaped not just policy, but culture.

Stewardship is the board's ability to integrate financial, strategical, technological, ethical, and societal outcomes into one conversation. It is no longer enough to sign off on profits; boards must also ask:

- *What is the human cost of our efficiency?*
- *What values do our algorithms enforce?*
- *Are we creating the future, or reacting to it?*

Boards that make this transition find that governance becomes less about limiting management and more about liberating responsible innovation. Stewardship is not about slowing innovation; it's about ensuring that speed doesn't outpace integrity.

The next competency is tech fluency. For decades, the gold standard for directors was financial literacy. But today, a perfectly balanced spreadsheet can hide an algorithmic disaster. The board of the future must be tech fluent, able to understand, question, and govern the technologies that now define competitiveness and risk.

This doesn't mean every director must be an engineer. But every director must know enough to ask the right questions:

- *How transparent is our AI decision-making?*
- *Where are our data vulnerabilities?*
- *Who is accountable for algorithmic bias or cybersecurity failures?*

When I began advising AI and technology ventures, I noticed how different their boardroom conversations were compared to legacy industries. They spent less time debating cost control and more time debating ethical control questions like, "*What does responsible scale look like?*" and "*Could we explain this decision to a regulator and a customer with equal clarity?*" Those questions weren't philosophical; they were strategic.

As boards mature, many are realizing that technology fluency without ethical fluency is incomplete. The future board must integrate tech and ethics and not treat them as parallel or delegated conversations. One AI platform company I studied recently created a Board Ethics & AI Subcommittee, intentionally designed to blend perspectives. Half of its members came from technology backgrounds, half from legal and social science fields. Their mandate was simple but demanding: review every high-impact system for fairness, privacy, and social impact before scale.

Within a year, that committee helped prevent two potential crises, one involving problematic data sourcing, another tied to automated decision bias. Nothing made headlines. No press release celebrated the restraint. Yet the outcome was tangible: investor confidence increased, customer trust deepened, and the company's market valuation rose. Not because of a breakthrough algorithm but because its governance signaled maturity and credibility.

Traditional boards are catching up. A financial services company I follow added a Technology & Trust Committee, chaired by a former regulator. Its role went far beyond reviewing IT budgets. The committee examined how data ethics, cybersecurity, and emerging technologies intersected with strategy, brand, and regulatory exposure. Within two years, this integrated approach became a competitive advantage. Clients increasingly viewed the company not just as innovative, but as safer and smarter to do business with.

The lesson is clear: technology risk is no longer purely technical, it is reputational. Boards that learn to connect technology decisions with ethical consequences will govern in the only currency that truly matters in the digital age: trust.

Technology literacy will soon be as fundamental to directors as audit literacy once was. And those who resist learning it will find themselves governing in the dark, while value, risk, and legitimacy are decided by systems they never truly understood.

Stewardship and technology fluency shape how boards govern, but they are ineffective without the right perspectives in the room. The next set of competencies determines whether boards can truly see the risks and opportunities ahead.

Global, Cognitive, and Geopolitical Diversity as Governance Capability

The third competency is often underestimated: global and cognitive diversity. Have you considered global and cognitive diversity as a resilient factor and Director competence? In my view, it is an important competence and includes geographic diversity, gender & generation diversity, professional diversity, geopolitical diversity and diversity of thought. A board that looks the same, thinks the same, and lives in the same geography cannot anticipate a world that doesn't. The future belongs to globally diverse boards, not just in identity, but in mindset.

A European industrial company I advised learned this lesson during expansion into Latin America. Their all-European board approved a marketing campaign that was well-received at home but sparked public outrage abroad for cultural insensitivity. Afterward, the company added directors from two of its fastest-growing markets, and every major initiative thereafter was reviewed through multiple cultural lenses. The difference was immediate: market share grew, reputational risks dropped, and internal pride soared.

Diversity isn't a checkbox; it's a risk mitigation strategy. It brings perspective, anticipation, and cultural fluency to complex global operations. Global diversity means a multitude of lens such as geographic diversity, gender & generational diversity, professional diversity and geopolitical diversity as explained below:

Geographic diversity gives boards early visibility into regional market shifts, regulatory change, and cultural dynamics that rarely appear in global dashboards until it is too late. Boards operating only from a single-country worldview miss the subtle and sometimes dramatic differences that shape risk, compliance, and opportunity across markets. A director who has operated in Europe reads regulatory signals differently from one who has built businesses in Southeast Asia or the Middle East. What looks like a product opportunity in the U.S. may trigger privacy concerns in Germany, nationalism in India, or data sovereignty constraints in Brazil. Someone who has navigated Southeast Asian markets will recognize when government partnerships accelerate expansion—or when local bureaucracy quietly slows it. A leader with experience in US understands sovereign expectations and national pride in ways that a purely Western board cannot.

Geographic diversity ensures the board can "see around corners" globally, not just locally anticipating where policies are tightening, where consumer sentiment is shifting, and where the company's next reputational exposure may emerge. It allows a company to anticipate regulatory shifts before they land in headlines: strengthening privacy rules in the EU, intensifying scrutiny of foreign ownership in APAC, rising consumer activism in Latin America, or new digital taxes across Africa. It is the difference between reading about a disruption and preparing for it.

If your board meets tomorrow to discuss expansion or a new technology rollout, whose lived experience would shape the conversation? Does your current composition help you "see around corners," or does it trap you inside a familiar worldview? In which regions are you making decisions without having a voice who knows the terrain first-hand?

Gender and generational diversity reshape how boards evaluate leadership, talent, and customers by broadening lived experience and challenging inherited assumptions. Gender and generational diversity represent internal and external stakeholder realities.

A board that mirrors the diversity of its workforce, customers, and communities gains access to insights that homogeneous groups routinely miss. Gender diversity often brings different perspectives on risk, culture, and customer behavior; generational diversity expands understanding of emerging technologies, talent expectations, and future markets. This isn't symbolism, it's strategy. When discussing issues like hybrid work, digital transformation, or inclusive product design, boards with diverse representation are far more grounded in the lived experience of the people they serve. They make fewer blind assumptions and more human-centered decisions.

Imagine a board debating hybrid work without a director who has managed early-career teams in the post-pandemic era. Or reviewing a new consumer product without someone who recognizes how Gen Z interprets brand authenticity. Diversity here is not a symbolic gesture, it is operational intelligence. Boards that include a wider range of lived experiences make decisions that resonate with the people who deliver and buy the company's products, rather than decisions optimized for the worldview of a few. In addition to be diverse, board members need to have the necessary competences and skills to serve and deliver a high-level performance

When your board debates culture, talent, or customer experience, whose reality is represented in the room? Are you hearing from the people who will actually use your product, join your workforce, or judge your ethics? Or are decisions being filtered through only one demographic lens?

Professional diversity prevents boards from governing through a single functional lens, enabling more balanced decisions across finance, technology, operations, and people. Professional diversity is relevant to balance entrepreneurial and institutional logic. High-performing boards blend operators, technologists, investors, entrepreneurs, and functional experts. Institutional leaders bring structure, risk management, and long-cycle thinking. Entrepreneurs bring creativity, velocity, and pattern recognition from environments where survival depends on rapid adaptation. Together, these voices create what I often describe as a "dynamic equilibrium"—bold enough to innovate, disciplined enough to scale. Professional diversity avoids the common blind spot where boards overweight finance or legal expertise while underestimating digital, operational, or cultural intelligence that is now required for modern decision-making.

Entrepreneurs pressure-test assumptions and inject creativity. Institutional leaders counterbalance with rigor, scenario planning, and governance discipline. Technologists challenge outdated models. Cultural or HR experts illuminate human implications that spreadsheets miss. It is this balance, not homogeneity, that prepares a board to guide companies through simultaneous waves of innovation and risk.

Look at your board composition today: *Do you have voices who know how to scale? Voices who know how to innovate? Voices who understand digital systems? Who is missing? And what risks arise because of that absence?*

Geopolitical diversity equips boards to navigate political risk, regulatory fragmentation, and societal expectations in an increasingly polarized world. Geopolitical diversity allows us to anticipate cross-border risks and keep global operations resilient. In an era defined by supply chain fragmentation, shifting alliances, sanctions regimes, and rising nationalism, geopolitical literacy is no longer optional. Boards need directors who understand the language of global risk, the signals behind tariffs, energy transitions, regional conflicts, and cross-border data regulations. A director with geopolitical depth helps the board recognize where instability might emerge and how it could cascade through distribution networks, talent flows, or market access. This diversity equips the board to make decisions that withstand global turbulence, not just domestic assumptions.

They understand not only what is happening, but why it is happening and how quickly it may escalate.

Boards that lack geopolitical literacy often react too late: factories shut down, suppliers vanish, logistics costs surge, or regulatory environments shift overnight. But boards with diverse geopolitical insight anticipate disruptions, design alternative sourcing routes, prepare compliance pathways, and build resilient partnerships long before a crisis strikes. The value is not theoretical, it shows up in continuity, credibility, and competitive advantage.

Who on your board truly understands the geopolitical forces shaping your supply chain, your markets, and your talent flows? How well are you positioned to make decisions if a regional conflict escalates, a trade barrier appears, or an AI rule changes cross-border data flows overnight?

Last but not the least diversity competence is the diversity of thought as a resilience factor. Diversity of thought activates all other forms of diversity by encouraging challenge, dissent, and constructive disagreement in the boardroom. True diversity goes beyond demographics, it's about diversity of thinking. The board of the future thrives on constructive dissent, not consensus theater.

A global logistics company I once followed during a transformation learned this when it brought in a behavioral economist to its board. She challenged long-held assumptions about efficiency and workforce incentives, reframing decisions that once seemed purely operational into human-centered ones. Within a year, productivity rose and employee turnover fell.

Diversity of thought creates tension, but it's the productive kind. It forces boards to test their assumptions under pressure before the market does it for them.

So, *do your board meetings include real disagreement or polite alignment? Is dissent welcomed, or quietly discouraged? Who in the room asks the questions that make others uncomfortable?*

Boards that encourage diverse thinking don't just avoid mistakes; they innovate through them.

Considering the resilient factor above, when boards are composed this way, discussions evolve from *"What's our exposure?"* to *"What's our opportunity?"*

Preparing the Workforce for the Age of Technology & AI: The Board's New Mandate

Technology and AI are transforming the workforce faster than any previous industrial shift. Yet most boards still treat workforce development as a "management initiative," reviewed annually instead of governed continuously. That approach is no longer viable. AI is not simply automating tasks, it is redefining decision rights, reconfiguring how teams operate, and altering what skills create value. Digital tools require digital fluency; predictive models require ethical judgment. Boards that fail to elevate workforce readiness to a strategic priority risk building advanced systems on a fragile human foundation. As a director, you must ask: *Are our people prepared for the future we are investing in or are we assuming they will figure it out alone?*

Equally important is how organizations integrate new generations into this transformation. Younger employees arrive with native digital intuition, high expectations for transparency, and a desire to understand not only what is changing but why. They want to see how technology aligns with purpose, culture, and fairness. Older employees bring industry judgment, reliability, and operational wisdom. When boards support environments where both groups learn from each other, productivity rises and transformation accelerates. But when boards fail to bridge these perspectives, companies end up with isolated pockets of expertise, internal friction, and resistance disguised as "change fatigue." In the age of AI and automation, intergenerational collaboration is not a cultural aspiration, it is an operational requirement.

No company can prepare its workforce alone. The scale and speed of technological transformation require coordinated ecosystems, schools, universities, vocational programs, community colleges, and government agencies working in tandem. I've seen how powerful these partnerships can be. For example, exposing engineering students to real-world AI and industrial challenges created a pipeline of talent that entered the workforce both curious and competent. I've witnessed similar progress when companies collaborate with state and local governments to build digital literacy programs for underserved communities. These partnerships are not philanthropy; they are strategic investments. Boards should encourage leadership to form these alliances proactively, ensuring talent pipelines remain strong and inclusive, and that communities evolve with technology rather than be left behind by it.

I've experienced the importance of this collaboration firsthand. A few years ago, while working with a global energy company and later with startups in the AI sector, I saw how employees at every level, from technicians to senior engineers, were eager to learn but unsure where to begin. We partnered with a local university to offer modular courses in AI fundamentals and digital operations. What surprised me most was not the increase in technical capability; it was the surge in morale. Employees felt valued, not threatened. A frontline worker told me, "No one ever invested in us like this before." That moment solidified a belief I now carry into every boardroom: workforce development is not a perk; it is a contract of trust.

Boards that treat workforce development as a strategic investment not a compliance exercise, create organizations capable of adapting, competing, and thriving through technological transformation.

Ask yourself and your board these uncomfortable but necessary questions: *Do we have a technology and AI talent strategy, or just a technology strategy? Are our people learning at the pace the business is changing? Who in this organization is being left behind and why? Do we partner meaningfully with universities, technical schools, and government programs, or do we expect talent to grow on its own? If our AI and technology plans succeed technically but fail culturally, what will it cost us?*

For directors, continuous education is a duty, not a bonus. In the old model, directors were appointed for what they knew. In the new model, they are valued for what they knew and for how fast they learn.

Technology cycles now outpace board cycles. A director can join a company fluent in today's operating model and be obsolete by next quarter's innovation. That reality has fundamentally changed the meaning of competence in the boardroom. The board of the future does not treat learning as optional or episodic; it institutionalizes learning as governance.

Some boards now schedule "learning blocks" into every quarterly meeting with dedicated briefings from external experts on AI, cybersecurity, geopolitics, or emerging markets. Others go further, organizing annual "tech immersions" where directors spend time in innovation hubs, universities, or startups to experience disruption firsthand rather than read about it in decks. In one global energy company where I observed governance reforms, the chair introduced a "reverse-mentoring" program. Younger digital leaders mentored board members on social media risk, data privacy, and generative AI. What emerged was not loss of authority, but mutual respect and a board culture that adapted faster because it listened better.

But learning alone is not enough. Boards cannot transform once and be done. The board of the future operates in cycles, reviewing, learning, adjusting, and recalibrating as the organization evolves. In one manufacturing group preparing for an IPO that I observed, the board created an internal "Governance Evolution Roadmap." It mapped where the board stood on issues such as technology literacy, ESG oversight, and cultural representation, and set clear targets for where it needed to be in three years. Progress was tracked with the same discipline as business KPIs. That roadmap became a mirror, forcing directors to evolve alongside the company. Within two years, the organization entered public markets with a reputation for forward-thinking governance, an advantage that impressed investors as much as its financial performance.

Future boards will not be static institutions. They will be learning ecosystems.

That shift is already being reinforced by the market. When Nasdaq announced its board diversity disclosure rule in 2021, the message was unmistakable: the legitimacy of corporate governance now includes representation. Companies must either meet baseline diversity expectations or publicly explain why they do not. The rule reframed diversity from moral aspiration to market expectation. Within 18 months, more than 75% of Nasdaq-listed companies reported new initiatives to diversify their boards or improve transparency. The impact went far beyond compliance. Boards began discussing culture, leadership pipelines, and inclusion with the same rigor they once reserved for finance and risk. Governance conversations started to include new questions: *Does our leadership reflect the customers we serve? Are we prepared to govern in markets where equality is policy, not preference?*

Nasdaq's move was not about quotas; it was about quality. It reminded directors that legitimacy today comes from visibility, accountability, and representation in the world they claim to serve.

Continuous learning, adaptive governance, and representative leadership are no longer future ambitions. They are present-day requirements. Because the next disruption, technological, ethical, or geopolitical will not wait for your next education session.

In your board, *when was the last time your board learned something together that materially changed a decision? Do you treat board education as an event or as a continuous system? If your board were assessed not only on what it oversees, but on how it evolves, what would the scorecard reveal? And most importantly: are you building a board designed to keep up or one designed to keep learning?*

Crisis Readiness as a Core Competence

Future boards must not just respond to crises; they must *rehearse* them.

One logistics firm in Europe now conducts "Crisis Simulations" twice a year, led by its board risk committee. Each simulation covers a different scenario: cyber breach, regulatory attack, social boycott. Every director participates.

The payoff? When a real data breach occurred, the company's response time was half that of its peers, and stakeholder confidence remained intact.

Crisis readiness builds muscle memory. It turns board meetings from theoretical discussions into real-time readiness.

Steering Mergers & IPOs in an Era Where Technology Redraws the Map

In the next decade, the most consequential decisions many boards will make will not be quarterly approvals, they will be transactions that define the company's future: mergers, acquisitions, divestitures, and IPOs. Historically, these events were anchored primarily in financial metrics and market timing. But the board of the future must navigate a far more complex landscape, where technology acceleration, AI maturity, cybersecurity risk, data governance, and shifting valuation models can make or break a deal.

M&A and IPO oversight now require tech fluency as much as financial fluency. A target company may look attractive on paper, strong revenue, promising growth but underneath may sit fragmented data infrastructures, outdated cybersecurity protocols, biased AI systems, or a technical debt so deep it could swallow integration synergies whole. Conversely, a young startup might appear overvalued until its AI capability, data assets, or network effects are properly understood. Boards must learn to read these signals as clearly as balance sheets.

The new due diligence is beyond the numbers. Future-ready boards expand due diligence beyond "what the company does" to "how the company works." That means interrogating:

1. AI Maturity & Data Infrastructure

- How modern is the company's technology stack?
- Are core processes automated, manual, or dependent on a few key individuals?
- Does the company own high-quality, clean, well-governed data or will integration require expensive rebuilding?

2. Cybersecurity & Digital Hygiene

- Are there undisclosed vulnerabilities or legacy systems waiting for exploitation?
- Is the company compliant with global data regulations (GDPR, CCPA, Brazil's LGPD, India's DPDP)?

3. Technical Debt & Integration Risk

- How much is hidden cost embedded in legacy systems?
- Would integration require rewiring the entire company?

4. AI & Algorithmic Risk

- Are algorithms explainable? Biased? Audited?
- Do they rely on third-party vendors that limit control?

5. Human Capital & Cultural Readiness

- Will the cultures integrate or collide?
- Can talent absorb a transformation that may accelerate immediately after the deal?

Currently, there is an increasing number of companies using technology not only to identify the opportunities and synergies values but also to unleash the value of target / acquired companies after the integration.

The board of the future understands that a merger can fail even when the financial case is strong because the technical or cultural foundation was weak.

The IPO Challenge: Readiness in a Market That Rewards (and Punishes) Technology

Going public used to be a test of financial rigor. Now it is a test of operational transparency, AI accountability, cybersecurity resilience, and data governance maturity. Analysts expect companies to demonstrate:

- Predictable data flows
- Cyber incident readiness

- AI guardrails and model documentation
- ESG and purpose integration
- Scalable digital infrastructure

Many companies underestimate this, believing they are preparing for a financial event when in reality, they are preparing for a transparency event.

As a Board member, you must ask can we withstand public scrutiny of our technology decisions? Do we have a repeatable operating cadence and not just a compelling story? Are we relying on heroics or on systems?

The IPO journey exposes every gap in governance, AI, cybersecurity, people, culture, ethics, controls, purpose. That's why future boards need to shape readiness years before filing.

Ask yourself and your board: *when we evaluate deals, do we evaluate code as seriously as we evaluate cash? Do we understand the AI, data, and cybersecurity risks we may inherit in a merger? Are we ready for the transparency and scrutiny that an IPO demands? Do we have directors with true digital, cybersecurity, or AI expertise or do we rely solely on management? Does our company technology can quickly be deployed to increase the synergies in our next M&A? How easily could our organization integrate another company's systems or be integrated itself? What assumptions are we making about valuation in a world where technology changes value overnight? Does our board encourage dissent when the financial story is compelling, but the technical risks are high?*

Boards that fail to ask these questions treat M&A like a spreadsheet exercise. Boards that succeed treat it like a strategic, technical, cultural, and ethical decision.

In the age of AI and digital dependence, the strongest boards are those that treat M&A and IPOs not as financial events but as technological commitments that demand courage, clarity, and deep governance discipline.

The Call to Action: Redefining the Modern Director

The question for every director today isn't whether the boardroom will evolve, it's whether you will. Technology is accelerating, geopolitics are shifting, AI is reshaping work, and M&A/IPO cycles demand an entirely new level of digital scrutiny. The boards that thrive will be those whose directors treat adaptation not as an aspiration, but as a personal mandate.

The board of the future will be defined by five traits that are no longer optional:

1. Stewardship as a Strategic Mindset - Tomorrow's board is not only accountable for financial results, but for workforce readiness, digital trust, and societal impact. AI will replace tasks, not purpose and boards must ensure that transformation benefits employees, customers, and communities. Stewardship is not charity; it is strategy.

2. Tech and Ethics Fluency - Not coding, comprehension. Directors must understand how AI influences behavior, how data shapes competitive advantage, how cybersecurity defines business continuity, and how ethical guardrails protect trust across borders. When your company acquires another business or prepares for an IPO, tech fluency becomes the margin between foresight and regret.

3. Global and Cognitive Diversity - Homogeneous boards miss the signals that matter. Geographic diversity helps navigate regulatory nuance; gender and generational diversity reveal blind spots in culture and talent; professional diversity blends entrepreneurial pace with institutional discipline. In a world where technology scales instantly but trust does not, diversity is not a virtue, it is a resilience mechanism.

4. Continuous Learning as a Fiduciary Duty - The half-life of expertise is shrinking. The board that does not learn together will fail together. Directors must treat education on AI, cybersecurity, regulation, workforce transformation, and geopolitical risk as seriously as audits and financial oversight.

5. Adaptive Governance - Governance frameworks cannot stay static in a world where technology, regulation, and business models shift monthly. The board of the future must refresh its structures, committees, metrics, and risk models the way leading companies update software continuously, consciously, and with intention.

Closing Reflection: What Future Are You Preparing Your Board For?

As you think about your own boardroom, pause and ask yourself:

When was the last time your board learned something new together? AI literacy session? Cyber drill? Workforce upskilling review?

Does your governance framework encourage reflection or resist it? Do you examine near-misses, blind spots, and cultural mismatches before they become crises?

Are your decisions built for a world where M&A, AI maturity, cybersecurity, and workforce readiness shape valuation as much as EBITDA? If a major acquisition landed on your agenda tomorrow, could your board probe the technology, not just the financials?

Are you preparing your workforce for the transformation you expect them to deliver? Or are you assuming talent will adapt without investment?

Do your decisions serve shareholders alone or the ecosystems that sustain them? Employees, communities, regulators, international partners, digital citizens?

The future of the boardroom will not be written by those who memorize the old rules. It will be written by those who are willing to rewrite them with curiosity, courage, and conscience. Because in the end, the board of the future is not a destination, it is a discipline.

A discipline of learning.

A discipline of stewardship.

A discipline of leading with integrity in a world where trust is the most valuable currency.

Chapter 11

The Leadership Virtues of the Future

Leadership is often measured by outcomes and composure, especially in the boardroom. Yet the most consequential moments of leadership are rarely planned or clearly labeled. They surface when courage is required without certainty, when curiosity matters more than expertise, when collaboration replaces authority, and when service, not self-interest, guides the decision. These moments do not appear in agendas or performance reviews, but they are the ones that ultimately define leadership.

Every leader believes they understand their values until a real test arrives. Maybe it's a crisis that exposes a blind spot. Maybe it's a market shift that demands uncomfortable decisions. Or maybe it's a quiet moment when you realize the next step in front of you is one you've never taken before.

That moment is where modern leadership begins.

The next decade will not reward leaders who rely on titles, hierarchy, or past success. It will reward those who can operate with courage, learn with curiosity, collaborate across boundaries, and serve with purpose. These are not soft attributes; they are survival skills in a world defined by disruption, AI acceleration, geopolitical uncertainty, and cultural fragmentation.

This chapter is written for board directors, founders, corporate executives, and entrepreneurial leaders who understand that leadership is being rewritten and who want to be part of that future rather than shaped by it.

By the end of this chapter, you will be equipped with four essential leadership virtues—practical, actionable, and battle-tested—and a framework to apply them in your own boardroom, startup, or community. Ask yourself as you read:

- *Where do I show courage and where do I hesitate?*
- *Am I still learning at the speed the world requires?*
- *Do I collaborate deeply or just cooperate politely?*
- *Who benefits from my leadership beyond my organization?*

The answers will define not just how you lead, but the legacy you leave.

The Four-Virtue Framework

1. Courage — acting with conviction before certainty

2. Curiosity & Ingenuity — learning with velocity. turning insight into inventive action.

3. Collaboration — building beyond silos

4. Service — leading for impact, not ego

These virtues reinforce one another.

- Courage sparks movement.
- Curiosity guides it.
- Ingenuity shapes it into solutions.
- Collaboration amplifies it.
- Service gives it meaning.

Together, they form a leadership architecture for the Interdependence Age, an era defined not by individual brilliance but by collective intelligence, shared stewardship, and adaptive learning. Boards and executives who cultivate all virtues create organizations capable not only of surviving disruption but shaping it responsibly.

The virtues are not traits, they are practices. What distinguishes enduring leaders from transactional managers is that these virtues are exercised regularly, not occasionally. Courage is built through repeated decisions that favor progress over perfection. Curiosity grows through disciplined learning and a willingness to question assumptions. Ingenuity strengthens through creative problem-solving under constraints. Collaboration expands as leaders intentionally build cross-sector, cross-culture, and cross-industry alliances. And service becomes authentic when practiced as stewardship, not performance. These are not personality traits; they are leadership muscles.

A framework for transformation, not inspiration. The virtue framework is not meant to inspire leaders; it is meant to orient them. In a world of accelerating AI disruption, geopolitical complexity, workforce redesign, and continuous reinvention, leaders require more than technical skills or governance structures. They need an integrated design for decision-making that aligns purpose, innovation, and responsibility. These virtues anchor that design. When applied consistently, they reshape cultures, elevate governance, and ensure that transformation is both bold and principled.

When boards and leaders embrace all five virtues, they build organizations capable of lasting transformation, enterprises that remain trusted, adaptive, and relevant in a world that demands nothing less.

1. Courage – The first Virtue of Transformation

Courage in leadership is rarely about heroics. More often, it's about taking one uncomfortable step when staying still feels safer.

Courage is the board that greenlights a strategic shift without full certainty.

Courage is the founder who admits a product isn't working.

Courage is the executive who challenges the status quo when the room wants continuity.

Courage Is Acting Before You Have All the Answers

In one multinational that I am familiar with, a major transformation stalled for two years because leadership feared announcing a bold digital strategy without perfect clarity. Competitors weren't waiting. By the time the company moved, market share had already eroded.

Contrast that with another organization: a global logistics operator that pivoted early to predictive automation during supply-chain turbulence. They didn't have full confidence, but they had conviction. Their courage paid off; they stabilized operations while peers scrambled.

A quiet form of courage. I've observed courage expressed in smaller, almost invisible ways too:

- A founder admitting she needed help scaling the business
- A board chair asking the CEO a difficult question in a calm, humane way
- An executive choosing what is right rather than what is easy

Courage is rarely dramatic. It's daily.

Ask yourself, *where in your leadership do you rely too heavily on certainty? What tough decision have you postponed and what is it costing your organization? Does your board reward courageous truth-telling or punish it?*

2. Curiosity & Ingenuity – The Leadership Superpowers Most Executives Underrate

If courage is the engine of transformation, curiosity is the fuel and ingenuity is the ignition that turns learning into action. Both are often spoken about but rarely understood as strategic capabilities for modern leadership.

Curiosity keeps leaders humble enough to learn, bold enough to experiment, and wise enough to avoid believing their own headlines. Ingenuity, in turn, enables them to convert what they learn into meaningful solutions. One opens the door; the other walks through it.

Curiosity and ingenuity are distinct but interconnected. Curiosity and ingenuity are frequently treated as synonyms, but they serve different roles in shaping visionary leaders:

Curiosity is the desire to explore, question, and understand. It pulls leaders toward new knowledge, technologies, cultures, perspectives, problems because something sparks wonder, complexity, or possibility. Curiosity drove the invention of the wheel, the development of agriculture, and the creation of the internet. It is the starting point of innovation, the mental spark that says: There must be something more here.

Ingenuity is the ability to apply that curiosity to create, combine, design, and solve. It is cleverness with intention, the skill of forming original combinations, devising inventive approaches, and navigating constraints with creativity. If curiosity asks, *"Why does this work?"* ingenuity asks, *"How can I make it better?"*

In summary, curiosity is the drive to learn and understand. Ingenuity is the ability to create and solve. Together, they form the foundation of human progress and leadership excellence.

My own career has been driven by curiosity, ingenuity and a little bit of planning. From global energy operations to entrepreneurship, AI governance, and startup boards, every major transition began with a simple question:

"What can I learn here?"

Curiosity becomes a competitive advantage because it is a discipline and not an accident. It manifests in leaders who:

- Explore new technologies before they are mainstream
- Engage deeply with cultures and viewpoints different from their own
- Ask questions that challenge familiar assumptions
- Seek future tension not just present comfort
- Build learning routines that create velocity, not stagnation

I recall a fast-growing Asian consumer brand once transformed its leadership pipeline by adopting a simple rule: every executive must demonstrate learning velocity. They tracked:

- New skills acquired
- Cross-functional exposure
- Experiments launched
- Peer-to-peer learning hours

This wasn't about academic credentials. It was about building curiosity into the operating system of leadership. The results were dramatic: innovation accelerated, silos dissolved, and curiosity became cultural currency.

Ingenuity Complements Curiosity. Curiosity alone is not enough. It gathers information—but ingenuity puts it to use. Leaders show ingenuity when they:

- Transform data into new business models
- Reimagine customer experiences with limited resources
- Connect dots across industries and geographies
- Build prototypes instead of presentations
- Solve constraints with creativity instead of capital

A curious leader says: *"There is a new technology emerging in this space."* An ingenious leader says: *"Here is how we can apply it to transform our operations, training, or customer experience."*

Curiosity opens possibilities. Ingenuity converts them into progress.

In an era of AI, geopolitical complexity, workforce redesign, and rapid industry transformation, leaders cannot rely on past knowledge. They must relearn how to learn and then creatively apply that learning. Executives who cultivate both curiosity and ingenuity become:

- Faster decision-makers
- More adaptive problem-solvers
- Stronger cross-cultural leaders
- Better board contributors
- More credible innovation champions

Curiosity prevents stagnation. Ingenuity prevents irrelevance.

Ask yourself, *when was the last time you learned something that genuinely challenged your worldview? What technology, trend, or market have you knowingly ignored and why? Are you modeling curiosity for your teams, or unintentionally outsourcing it to "innovation groups"? When was the last time you solved a problem creatively rather than procedurally?*

Do you gather knowledge without converting it into action, or do you consistently turn insight into innovation? How does your organization reward curiosity and how does it reward ingenuity? What new skill, emerging technology, or market shift will you intentionally explore this year? Where can you demonstrate greater learning velocity? Where can you demonstrate greater inventive problem-solving?

3. Collaboration - The Power Skill of the Interdependence Age

The world's biggest challenges—AI governance, supply-chain fragility, climate adaptation, global expansion—cannot be solved by single organizations. Collaboration is not an option; it is a strategic multiplier. Collaboration is not consensus.

High-performing collaborators:

- Challenge constructively
- Share information proactively
- Build coalitions across competitors, industries, and cultures
- View knowledge as a collective asset

I once followed a cross-industry alliance between three companies from Asia, Europe, and Latin America, each struggling with a different challenge—data privacy, inclusion, and regulatory fragmentation. They discovered that collaboration offered what internal teams could not: combined intelligence, shared learning, and global context.

The unexpected outcome? Their joint framework became the gold standard for a regional regulatory body. This is collaboration at its highest form, not cooperation, but co-creation.

In another example, a startup developing global API infrastructure could not scale because of fragmented regulations. Instead of fighting alone, the founders created a working group with customers, regulators, and competitors. The result? A shared compliance framework that unlocked expansion in 20+ markets.

Collaboration requires maturity, not harmony. One of the most misunderstood aspects of collaboration is the belief that it requires harmony or alignment at all times. In reality, meaningful collaboration is often loud, uncomfortable, and filled with productive tension. Mature leaders understand that friction is not a sign of failure, it is evidence that diverse viewpoints are being surfaced and integrated. This tension sharpens strategy, exposes blind spots, and accelerates innovation. Collaboration thrives not when everyone agrees, but when everyone is committed to a shared purpose strong enough to withstand disagreement.

The ecosystem advantage is winning through interdependence. Today's most resilient organizations no longer think in terms of linear value chains; they think in ecosystems. When companies tap into universities, startups, regulators, nonprofits, and global industry groups, they amplify their reach and relevance. Ecosystem leadership means understanding that competitive advantage often emerges *between* organizations, not within them. In sectors like AI, cybersecurity, energy, and healthcare, no single player can keep pace alone. Leaders who embrace interdependence unlock network effects with access to talent, data, insights, and markets that no one company could build on its own.

Collaboration is scale.

Are you collaborating broadly or just with people who think like you? What could your organization achieve if it partnered across sectors? Is your leadership rewarding silo behavior or ecosystem behavior? What expertise or perspectives are missing from your current collaboration networks and why haven't they been included yet? When was the last time you initiated a partnership that felt uncomfortable or unfamiliar? Which problem in your organization today could be solved faster or better through shared ownership rather than internal escalation? Are you building an ecosystem that will still matter five years from now or one that only serves immediate needs?

4. Service – The Virtue That Defines Leaders Who Are Remembered

Service is the culminating virtue because courage, curiosity, and collaboration mean little unless anchored in purpose. Service Is Not Charity. It Is Stewardship.

Service in leadership means that decisions consider:

- Employees
- Communities
- Customers
- Suppliers
- Future generations

It is about lifting others, developing talent, and driving impact beyond spreadsheets.

Patagonia's decision to transfer ownership to fight climate change reframed corporate stewardship globally. Boards realized that Purpose can coexist with profit when service is authentic.

Personally, one of my most rewarding activities servicing the communities is called "Haircuts with Heart". As a multi-brand franchisee of one of the largest hair salon franchisors, our company have partnered with several children's hospitals in Houston, March of Dimes and Ronald Foundation and bring volunteer hair stylists to support NICU families with free haircuts. We convert a hospital room in a hair salon and for half day, we bring a happy moment to NICU babies' families. It is simple, heartfelt, and profoundly appreciated not only by the community but also by the employees. And it taught me this:

Communities remember leaders who show up. Not leaders who show off.

Service Is a strategic lens, and an act of kindness. In the modern boardroom, service is becoming a strategic differentiator. Organizations that adopt a service-led mindset make decisions with broader systems in mind: environmental impact, workforce well-being, long-term societal outcomes, and the ripple effects of innovation. This lens stretches leaders beyond transactional thinking and into transformational leadership. It reframes the question from "What must we deliver?" to "What must we protect, uplift, and enable?" When service becomes part of decision-making, governance shifts from short-term optimization to long-term stewardship.

The paradox of service is that power grows when shared. What many executives overlook is that service is not a subtraction of authority; it is a multiplication of influence. When leaders invest in people, communities, and ecosystems, they build a reservoir of trust. Trust becomes resilience during crises, credibility during transitions, and strength during reinvention. Service is ultimately an exercise in empowerment giving others the tools, confidence, and opportunities to succeed. Leaders who serve create leaders who serve. This is what builds legacies that last beyond titles and tenures.

Why Service Strengthens Governance

Boards that cultivate service-led governance:

- Attract stronger talent
- Maintain stakeholder trust
- Build reputational resilience
- See beyond quarterly cycles

Ask yourself, *who benefits from your leadership decisions? How often do you consider the community impact of governance choices? What legacy do you want your leadership to leave? When have you used your influence to elevate someone with less power or visibility? Whose voice is missing from your leadership table, and what responsibility do you have to bring it forward? Are your company's community efforts integrated into strategy—or treated as side projects? In moments of pressure, do you default to protecting the organization—or serving the broader ecosystem that sustains it?*

Closing Reflection — The Leadership Legacy You Choose

In a world defined by volatility and acceleration, your greatest competitive advantage is not your title, your experience, or your company's balance sheet. It is your values.

Courage to make the first move. Curiosity to learn the next insight.

Ingenuity to transform learning into action. Collaboration to build beyond yourself. Service to ensure your leadership matters.

If you embrace these virtues, you will not only lead effectively, you will lead meaningfully.

Leadership legacies are rarely defined by dramatic decisions or headline-making achievements. They are shaped in smaller, quieter moments in how you treat people when no one is watching, what you choose to prioritize during busy seasons, and whether you uphold your principles when convenience suggests otherwise. These unseen choices accumulate into reputation, trust, and ultimately influence. Long after strategies change and titles fade, what remains is the imprint you left on people and institutions.

The leaders who will be remembered in the decades ahead are those who blend human depth with adaptive capacity. Technologies will accelerate, markets will shift, and governance models will evolve but the ability to stay grounded in values while navigating complexity will distinguish those who endure. Ingenuity will help you innovate; curiosity will help you grow, courage will help you act, collaboration will help you scale, and service will keep your leadership anchored in purpose rather than ego. This balance, humanity plus adaptability, is the hallmark of modern leadership.

As you reflect about the virtues of courage, curiosity, ingenuity, collaboration, and service into your daily leadership practice. Reflect on them individually, or bring them into board discussions, team offsites, or personal journaling. *Where am I hesitating because I want certainty rather than progress? What decision would I make if fear were not the primary voice in the room? What assumptions have I not questioned in the past six months? Which emerging trend, technology, or perspective have I avoided exploring? Where can I apply an inventive solution instead of relying on familiar methods? What constraints could become catalysts for innovation if reframed intentionally? Who outside my immediate circle should be part of my next strategic conversation? What partnership could unlock exponential value not just incremental benefit? Who benefits from my leadership today and who should benefit tomorrow? How will I ensure that my influence uplifts more people than it protects?*

Leadership is a choice you renew every day, not a role you inherit. Long after dashboards are replaced, strategies revised, and markets redefined, your leadership will be remembered for its humanity, its courage, and its willingness to evolve. You write your legacy not through authority, but through the moments when you choose learning over certainty, ingenuity over complacency, collaboration over isolation, and service over ego.

The future does not belong to the boldest voice or the loudest brand. It belongs to the leaders who remain grounded, curious, inventive, and committed to something larger than themselves. In your boardroom, in your company, in your community, you are shaping the world that others will inherit.

Write it with intention.

Appendix A

Governance Reflection Questions

A Living Checklist for Leaders, Boards, and Founders

This appendix brings together the reflection questions from each chapter of *Boarding the Future*. These questions are designed to be revisited over time—before major decisions, during periods of disruption, and as part of ongoing board and leadership development.

They are not theoretical. They are intended to surface blind spots, challenge assumptions, and strengthen governance judgment in real-world contexts.

You may use them:

- Individually, for personal leadership reflection
- In board evaluations and governance reviews
- During strategy offsites and transformation checkpoints
- As prompts for founder–board or executive–board dialogue

Chapter 1 — The New Governance Mandate

Leading in an Age of AI, Acceleration, and Global Complexity

- Is our governance system built for the world we are entering or the one we are leaving behind?
- Do we understand AI deeply enough to govern it responsibly, not just approve it strategically?
- Where has speed outpaced oversight in our organization?
- Are we balancing startup agility with legacy discipline or defaulting to one at the expense of the other?

- What governance risks worry us privately but rarely appear in board materials?
- Which era of governance does your board most resemble today, and which risks does that leave ungoverned?
- Where are algorithms, platforms, or automated systems already making decisions faster than your board reviews them?
- Does your governance model prioritize learning, or does it reward certainty and precedent?
- Where is your organization relying on resilience it hopes it has, rather than resilience it has designed?
- If a major AI or reputational incident occurred tomorrow, would your board know who is accountable within hours or days?
- What decisions in your organization are already being made without meaningful human oversight?
- Which risks are invisible to your current governance structure?
- Are you governing for the past or for the systems now shaping your future?

Chapter 2 — Entrepreneurial Agility - What Startups Teach Leaders About Speed, Learning, and Focus

- Where are we debating instead of deciding?
- How quickly do insights from customers reach the boardroom?
- Do we reward experimentation—or only success?
- What decision could we safely make faster if accountability were clearer?

- Which startup behaviors would most improve our governance velocity in the next 90 days?
- How long does it take for your board or leadership team to make a meaningful decision? Weeks? Months?
- Imagine competing against a startup that decides in hours. Could your team pivot that fast if the market changes tomorrow? How would you respond?
- If your company faces a sudden market shock tomorrow, could your leadership team pivot within days?
- Would your board tolerate a failed pilot project as a step toward learning? Or would that failure be punished and buried?
- Do your executives know how to treat experiments as data, not disasters?
- What would your organization do differently if your budget were cut in half tomorrow?
- Would you collapse under the weight of lost resources, or would you focus on what truly creates value?
- Is your board governing as if you have unlimited time and certainty? Or are you building systems that can withstand shocks, pivot under pressure, and sustain performance when the ground shifts beneath you?
- Does your board allow management to place small bets, or do you demand certainty before action?
- Does your board know who your real customers are and are their voices shaping decisions?
- When was the last time that your Board talked directly to some of the customers?
- Does your organization treat cash as a strategic enabler—or as an afterthought?

- Do your oversight practices slow innovation, or do they enable it by providing disciplined trust?
- Does your board still measure success only in financial terms, or are you building a culture of adaptability?
- Do your executives fear failure, or do they see it as feedback?
- Does your governance framework assume one size fits all? Or are you adjusting to cultural context when you expand across borders?

Chapter 3 — Resilience from Legacy Industries - Discipline, Redundancy, and Long-Cycle Thinking

- What happens when stability becomes the exception, not the rule?
- What lessons from those legacy organizations could make your own company stronger? Could you borrow their discipline without inheriting their bureaucracy? Could you apply their risk mindset without slowing down your innovation?
- In your organization, do you see discipline as bureaucracy, or as the backbone of resilience?
- In times of disruption, would your systems hold under stress or collapse because you treated discipline as optional?
- Have you mapped the hidden stakeholders in your ecosystem—beyond shareholders—who could define your resilience in crisis? Are you governing in a way that balances their competing expectations?
- In your organization, do you cut buffers in the name of efficiency, or do you recognize them as strategic insurance?
- Is your board treating reputation as a line item on risk registers or as a core asset to be protected and invested in?

- Does your startup strategize how to build its reputation?
- Do your systems allow you to flex both ways or are you only built for growth in good times?
- If demand dropped 30% tomorrow, could your organization downshift with discipline rather than panic?
- Are your executives under pressure to move fast without safety nets?
- Does your governance system elevate discipline to the same level as growth targets?
- Have you defined your true stakeholders or are you still listening only to shareholders and quarterly earnings?
- As a founder, have you truly identified your stakeholders?
- What if your supply chain is cut off tomorrow?
- What if your flagship technology is leapfrogged?
- What if a funding round falls through?
- Is your organization planning only for growth or are you rehearsing survival and reinvention?
- As a startup founder, have you identified the entire market potential and run the what ifs?
- Are your executives rewarded for short-term efficiency at the expense of long-term resilience?
- Does your leadership treat reputation as a strategic asset, or as an afterthought to earnings calls and pitch decks?
- Are your partnerships built for shared growth or shared resilience?
- Do your board's governance triggers signal when to slow down as confidently as they do when to grow? Does your board's governance framework indicate when to slow down

with the same clarity and confidence that it signals when to pursue growth?

- Does your organization's model of resilience fit its cultural and economic context?
- Have you learned from how others across the globe survive disruption differently?
- Do you have a strategic approach for your startup reputation?
- Is resilience part of your governance culture or just a crisis plan in a binder?
- if tomorrow brought another shock a market crash, a supply breakdown, or a technology failure, would your organization bend and recover, or would it fracture under the weight of surprise?
- What habits of governance, what investments in people, what reserves of trust are you building today to withstand that test?
- Where are we mistaking efficiency for resilience?
- What single-point failures would hurt us most if disrupted tomorrow?
- Have we stress-tested our assumptions beyond optimistic scenarios?
- Are we building redundancy intentionally—or discovering it accidentally in crisis?
- What discipline from legacy industries should we reclaim before the next shock?

Chapter 4 — The Board and AI Oversight: Balancing Innovation and Accountability

- Does your board treat AI as a strategic priority with time, debate and dissent or as an occasional update from the CIO?

- Do your governance systems balance innovation with accountability or rely on luck to stay compliant?
- Does your board treat AI as a line item or as a strategic capability?
- When you hear "automation," do you also hear "accountability"?
- If an AI system made a contested decision yesterday, denied a loan, rejected a résumé, flagged a safety incident, would your board even know?
- Would you know who owns accountability when that decision is challenged?
- Can your board explain, in one sentence, how AI is used in your organization and who is accountable for it?
- Would you know if it (your AI system) failed?
- Does your organization know which AI systems pose high risk?
- Are you proportioning oversight to impact, or treating all AI the same? Do your governance documents, committee charters, reporting lines and escalation paths, reflect this new reality?
- If your board adopted a tiered AI review tomorrow, which systems would qualify for top-tier scrutiny and who would decide?
- Could you defend your oversight to a regulator tomorrow?
- When your board approves AI spending, are you endorsing a technology or a purpose-driven outcome?
- If your algorithm could answer the question "What does winning look like?", would its definition match your organization's values? And most importantly, is AI embedded in your enterprise strategy or orbiting outside it, unaligned and unexamined?

- Does your culture allow people to question AI outcomes openly?
- How do you reward curiosity and caution?
- Do your employees know when to escalate concerns and that they'll be heard when they do?
- If an AI system in your organization caused harm tomorrow, could you trace responsibility?
- Does your audit committee review algorithmic risks, or only financial ones?
- Are your governance structures clear enough for accountability to survive leadership transitions?
- Are your metrics clear and sufficient to estimate and measure the investment ROI?
- Where in your organization does innovation die under "big bet" theater, and where could small, instrumented bets move you faster with less risk?
- If your top model provider turned off access tomorrow, what would break and what have you already done to make sure "everything" is not the answer?
- Does your AI policy travel well across borders, or does it assume one-size-fits-all?
- Have you defined what "responsible AI" means in your cultural context?
- If your company operated in a country with stricter or looser AI norms, would your governance still hold?
- Does your board have an AI readiness plan that's as robust as your cybersecurity framework?
- When you hear the term machine learning, do you think of opportunity or liability?

- Are you building a governance system that reacts to errors or one that prevents them?
- If tomorrow's headlines named your company in an AI-related incident, could you confidently explain your safeguards to investors, regulators, and the public?
- Did you use AI to act with speed and integrity, or did you let automation decide in your name?
- Are we monitoring AI or truly governing it?
- Can we clearly explain what our most critical algorithms optimize for?
- Who is accountable when an AI system fails or causes harm?
- How visible is AI risk to the board compared to financial risk?
- Would we be prepared to explain an AI failure publicly—tomorrow?

Chapter 5 — Right-Sized Governance Enables Startups to Scale and Corporates to Innovate Without Losing Control

- Is your board creating clarity and velocity, or complexity and drag?
- If you removed half your governance tomorrow, what would break?
- If you doubled it, what would stall?
- Is your governance designed to enable your organization's next stage of growth, or is it trapping you in its last?
- Would your current governance frameworks survive if stretched across three continents? Or would they collapse under the weight of complexity?

- Does your board treat time as infinite?
- Do your executives believe they have months or years to adapt to disruption?
- If your board received an activist letter tomorrow, could you defend your plan with data and conviction or would you scramble to craft the narrative you should already have told?
- Are your global risks integrated or scattered across disconnected updates?
- When crises hit, does your governance default to compliance and defense or can you balance transparency, accountability, and strategy in the same breath?
- Does your private company board have a plan for succession or is it relying on assumptions that leadership will "figure it out" later?
- If your enterprise had to expand internationally tomorrow, would your tax, legal, and governance structures hold or would they collapse under local complexity?
- Is your governance system flexible enough to balance founder vision, family priorities, and investor expectations without gridlock?
- Do you treat governance as a strategic enabler, or simply as a family obligation?
- Does your non-profit board spend enough time managing credibility, not just cash?
- Do your governance systems protect not only your programs but your reputation for fairness and integrity?
- If you lifted your non-profit into another cultural context tomorrow, which values would remain constant, and which practices would you adapt? Is that written down?

- Which compass point is weakest in your board today? If you strengthened just that one over the next 90 days, what would change?
- Which practice from "the other world" would most help you in the next 90 days—and who on your board will champion it?
- Startup: Are you over-rotating to vision and under-rotating to cash? What one governance ritual would save you from a preventable failure?
- Public: What single page would convince an activist to invest rather than attack?
- Private: If your founder became unavailable tomorrow, who steps in—and what would the first 30 days look like?
- Non-Profit: Are you measuring what donors want and what communities value? Where is trust fragile?
- If you had to defend your cross-border practices to a skeptical regulator next week, who would speak, what would they show, and how quickly could they assemble it?
- Is your governance a source of energy or exhaustion?
- Where is the smallest intervention that would create the largest improvement?
- Who on your board will own the experiment to right-size governance in the next 60 days?
- Where has governance become friction instead of enablement?
- Where does lack of structure create unnecessary risk?
- Is your governance proportional to impact or copied from unrelated models?
- What governance ritual could we simplify without increasing risk?

- What governance capability must evolve next as we scale?
- Chapter 6 — Risk, Ethics, Regulatory and Trust in AI
- What human judgment have you replaced with AI and what principles must remain?
- If your algorithm made tomorrow's front page, would it represent your purpose or betray it?
- Are you governing AI as a tool for scale or as a mirror of your company's values?
- Are your board's AI oversight tools scaled to the actual risk of each system, or are they blanket policies that create blind spots?
- When your AI models act faster than governance can respond, what safeguards ensure they never act beyond your values?
- Do your board packs translate AI risk into business impact or just technical jargon?
- Is accountability for AI decisions explicit, documented, and auditable?
- Does your board receive AI risk metrics alongside financial KPIs?
- Can management explain a model failure in one slide without jargon?
- When was your last AI incident simulation?
- How do lessons learned update board policy in real time?
- Does your board track upcoming AI legislation by region and industry?
- Who in your company is responsible for interpreting and harmonizing these frameworks?

- Are you designing AI governance to meet regulations or to shape it?
- If your company were audited tomorrow under the EU AI Act or NIST RMF, could you produce the evidence regulators would expect?
- Which compass point—clarity, cadence, candor, or calibration—is weakest in your AI oversight?
- How would your governance rhythm change if AI were treated as both a risk and an opportunity engine?
- If an AI failure strikes your organization tomorrow, would your board be ready to explain, to act, and to rebuild trust? Or would you still be drafting a policy while the headlines write themselves?
- Do we treat ethics as compliance—or as strategy?
- Where could automation bias undermine trust in our decisions?
- Are ethical risks discussed with the same rigor as financial risks?
- Can our governance frameworks recover trust after failure—or only prevent it?
- How do we measure trust as a living asset, not a slogan?

Chapter 7 — Global Adaptability as a Strategic Edge

- How fluent are you in local context?
- When was the last time your global strategy truly reflected regional insight rather than corporate instinct?

- Does your organization's strategy adapt to different cultural and regulatory contexts or assume one size fits all?

- How well does your board anticipate geopolitical shifts that could reshape supply, data, or talent flows?

- Do you have voices around the table who can translate between markets between speed and caution, scale and sensitivity?

- Does your leadership team reflect true global fluency, not just global presence?

- When your board debates transformation, do you weigh local nuance as carefully as financial return?

- Which rhythm dominates your boardroom—speed, caution, consensus, or resilience?

- How do you adapt your governance cadence when entering a new market? Do you have directors who can translate between these worlds not just linguistically, but strategically?

- How much time do you talk about global adaptability to the company initiatives?

- Does your organization assume disruption moves at one speed?

- Are you testing global strategies against local expectations?

- When entering new markets, do you listen first or lead with assumptions?

- When you reflect about your company or your board, who in your organization acts as your cultural interpreter?
- Do your KPIs reward global insight or local imitation?
- How often does your leadership test ideas with cross-border teams before execution?
- Boards should challenge management with questions such as how does this strategy translate across cultures? Have we pressure-tested assumptions against local behavior? Do we have the right voices in the room to challenge "home-country bias"?
- When your global strategy fails, is it execution or empathy?
- Who, in your boardroom, speaks to the customer in Jakarta or Johannesburg?
- Does your governance model allow variation or enforce uniformity that stifles progress?
- Are we designing AI that respects local norms, regulations, and expectations or are we allowing technology to collide with culture?
- Are we building organizations that adapt to the world or expect the world to adapt to us?
- Who in our leadership team acts as a cultural and regulatory interpreter?
- How often do we test assumptions before exporting strategies globally?

- Does our AI or technology reflect local norms—or collide with them?

- Where could global misalignment turn into reputational risk?

Chapter 8 — The Transformation Playbook for Executives

Vision × Talent × Governance × Execution

- Is your organization talking about transformation or living it?
- When disruption hits, does your team move with clarity or with confusion?
- Are you building a transformation story, or a transformation system?
- Can every person in your organization explain why transformation matters now?
- Does your vision connect to both global trends (AI, digitalization, sustainability) and local realities (culture, regulation, behavior)?
- When you speak about transformation, do people feel urgency—or fatigue?
- Who in your organization is shaping the future, and who is anchoring it?
- Are your reward systems built for stability or for learning?
- Does your transformation budget allocate more to technology than to talent? If so, invert it.
- Can your frontline teams clearly see how their work connects to your company's transformation story or are they still guessing what the vision really means?

- If you walked into a project meeting tomorrow, would people speak in the language of alignment or activity?
- Does your transformation roadmap translate into visible progress every quarter or does it linger in presentations no one revisits?
- Are you measuring outcomes that people can feel—customer satisfaction, speed, engagement—or just internal outputs and activity?
- How many of your "strategic priorities" have actually reached the customer?
- As a board member, have you mapped your stakeholders by both power and passion?
- How are you communicating trade-offs transparently?
- When disruption hits, who hears from you first—the investors or the employees?
- Are your transformation metrics telling a story of progress or of activity without impact?
- Do they measure what truly changes for your customers, employees, and stakeholders, or just what gets reported?
- When was the last time your board reviewed not just the pace of transformation, but the confidence behind it?
- What would your Transformation Dashboard show if published publicly tomorrow?
- Which metrics reflect learning and trust, not just output?
- How can your board create safe spaces for experimentation without losing oversight?
- Do your governance systems reward learning or only punish failure?

- When was the last time your leadership team admitted, "We don't know, let's test"?
- Do your board meetings celebrate progress or only perfection?
- If your organization faced another global shock tomorrow, would you improvise or be ready?
- What part of your playbook still lives in slides and what part already beats in behavior?
- Is our transformation roadmap producing visible progress each quarter?
- Are we measuring outcomes people can feel—or just outputs we can report?
- Do our governance guardrails enable speed—or slow it?
- Where does execution break down despite strong strategy?
- What part of transformation still lives in slides instead of behavior?

Chapter 9 — The Startup Governance Playbook

- Is your board a partner or a referee?
- Do your investors challenge strategy or only react to results?
- Are you building a company that can govern itself when you're not in the room?
- Are your advisors empowered to challenge you or just to cheer you on?
- Do you track decisions or rely on memory?
- How often do your investors hear from you between funding rounds?
- Are you coachable and agile to quickly adapt to the market requirements?

- Does your board have the right skills or just familiar faces?
- Are you spending more time justifying the past quarter or shaping the next one?
- Have you defined when decisions need board approval and when they don't?
- Do your committees reflect today's risks or yesterday's structure?
- Can your governance scale globally without adding friction?
- If your board meeting minutes were published tomorrow, would they build confidence or concern?
- Do your board meetings feel like performance reviews or strategy sessions?
- Are dissenting voices valued or avoided?
- Is your board composition built for your next stage or your last round?
- Do you listen to your board?
- Periodically audit your board by asking key questions such as does our structure fit our current risk profile? Are our meetings focused on learning or reporting? Are we spending time on what drives enterprise value or what's easy to measure? Which skills and expertise do we need to add to the board?
- How transparent are your financials to investors and employees?
- When decisions go wrong, do you blame or learn?
- Does your board measure trust or just targets?
- Have you designed your board to make you better or to make you comfortable?

- Do your directors know your blind spots and are they empowered to call them out?
- Is your governance evolving faster than your business?
- Does your startup have the governance it deserves or just the governance it inherited?
- If tomorrow brought a crisis—funding shortfall, compliance issue, reputational risk—would your board be ready to lead, or would it freeze?
- Are you building a company that will outlast your energy and your ownership?
- Is governance helping us move faster—or making us hesitate?
- Do founder and board roles feel like partnership or surveillance?
- Have we formalized accountability at the right moment—or too late?
- Where do advice and authority blur dangerously?
- What governance decision today would investors reward tomorrow?

Chapter 10 — The Board of the Future

- Which type of board are you on today, the one already evolving, the one learning under pressure, or the one still waiting?
- Does your board operate as a quarterly review committee or as a strategic nerve center?
- When technology or ethics enters the conversation, does the room lean in or tune out?
- If your organization were judged tomorrow on the

transparency, fairness, and foresight of its decisions, would your board be ready or exposed?

- What is the human cost of our efficiency?
- What values do our algorithms enforce?
- Are we creating the future, or reacting to it?
- How transparent is our AI decision-making?
- Where are our data vulnerabilities?
- Who is accountable for algorithmic bias or cybersecurity failures?
- If your board meets tomorrow to discuss expansion or a new technology rollout, whose lived experience would shape the conversation?
- Does your current composition help you "see around corners," or does it trap you inside a familiar worldview?
- In which regions are you making decisions without having a voice who knows the terrain first-hand?
- When your board debates culture, talent, or customer experience, whose reality is represented in the room?
- Are you hearing from the people who will actually use your product, join your workforce, or judge your ethics? Or are decisions being filtered through only one demographic lens?
- Do you have voices who know how to scale? Voices who know how to innovate? Voices who understand digital systems? Who is missing? And what risks arise because of that absence?
- Who on your board truly understands the geopolitical forces shaping your supply chain, your markets, and your talent flows?

- How well are you positioned to make decisions if a regional conflict escalates, a trade barrier appears, or an AI rule changes cross-border data flows overnight?
- Do your board meetings include real disagreement or polite alignment?
- Is dissent welcomed, or quietly discouraged?
- Who in the room asks the questions that make others uncomfortable?
- Do we have a technology and AI talent strategy, or just a technology strategy?
- Are our people learning at the pace the business is changing?
- Who in this organization is being left behind and why?
- Do we partner meaningfully with universities, technical schools, and government programs, or do we expect talent to grow on its own?
- If our AI and technology plans succeed technically but fail culturally, what will it cost us?
- Does our leadership reflect the customers we serve?
- Are we prepared to govern in markets where equality is policy, not preference?
- When was the last time your board learned something together that materially changed a decision?
- Do you treat board education as an event or as a continuous system?
- If your board were assessed not only on what it oversees, but on how it evolves, what would the scorecard reveal?
- Are you building a board designed to keep up or one designed to keep learning?

- When we evaluate deals, do we evaluate code as seriously as we evaluate cash?
- Do we understand the AI, data, and cybersecurity risks we may inherit in a merger?
- Are we ready for the transparency and scrutiny that an IPO demands?
- Do we have directors with true digital, cybersecurity, or AI expertise or do we rely solely on management?
- Does our company technology can quickly be deployed to increase the synergies in our next M&A?
- How easily could our organization integrate another company's systems or be integrated itself?
- What assumptions are we making about valuation in a world where technology changes value overnight?
- Does our board encourage dissent when the financial story is compelling, but the technical risks are high?
- When was the last time your board learned something new together? AI literacy session? Cyber drill? Workforce upskilling review?
- Does your governance framework encourage reflection or resist it?
- Do you examine near-misses, blind spots, and cultural mismatches before they become crises?
- Are your decisions built for a world where M&A, AI maturity, cybersecurity, and workforce readiness shape valuation as much as EBITDA? If a major acquisition landed on your agenda tomorrow, could your board probe the technology, not just the financials?
- Are you preparing your workforce for the transformation you expect them to deliver? Or are you assuming talent will adapt without investment?

- Do your decisions serve shareholders alone or the ecosystems that sustain them? Employees, communities, regulators, international partners, digital citizens?
- Does our board reflect the markets and communities we serve?
- Are we learning together as a board—or relying on outdated expertise?
- How fluent are we in technology risk beyond financial exposure?
- Would a new generation of leaders see this board as credible?
- Are we governing change or reacting to it?

Chapter 11 — The Leadership Virtues of the Future

- Where do I show courage and where do I hesitate?
- Am I still learning at the speed the world requires?
- Do I collaborate deeply or just cooperate politely?
- Who benefits from my leadership beyond my organization?
- Where in your leadership do you rely too heavily on certainty?
- What tough decision have you postponed and what is it costing your organization?
- Does your board reward courageous truth-telling or punish it?
- When was the last time you learned something that genuinely challenged your worldview?
- What technology, trend, or market have you knowingly ignored and why?
- Are you modeling curiosity for your teams, or unintentionally outsourcing it to "innovation groups"?

- When was the last time you solved a problem creatively rather than procedurally?
- Do you gather knowledge without converting it into action, or do you consistently turn insight into innovation?
- How does your organization reward curiosity and how does it reward ingenuity?
- What new skill, emerging technology, or market shift will you intentionally explore this year?
- Where can you demonstrate greater learning velocity?
- Are you collaborating broadly or just with people who think like you?
- What could your organization achieve if it partnered across sectors?
- Is your leadership rewarding silo behavior or ecosystem behavior?
- What expertise or perspectives are missing from your current collaboration networks and why haven't they been included yet?
- When was the last time you initiated a partnership that felt uncomfortable or unfamiliar?
- Which problem in your organization today could be solved faster or better through shared ownership rather than internal escalation?
- Are you building an ecosystem that will still matter five years from now or one that only serves immediate needs?
- Where can you demonstrate greater inventive problem-solving?
- Who benefits from your leadership decisions?

- How often do you consider the community impact of governance choices?
- What legacy do you want your leadership to leave?
- When have you used your influence to elevate someone with less power or visibility?
- Whose voice is missing from your leadership table, and what responsibility do you have to bring it forward?
- Are your company's community efforts integrated into strategy or treated as side projects?
- In moments of pressure, do you default to protecting the organization or serving the broader ecosystem that sustains it?
- Where am I hesitating because I want certainty rather than progress?
- What decision would I make if fear were not the primary voice in the room?
- What assumptions have I not questioned in the past six months?
- Which emerging trend, technology, or perspective have I avoided exploring?
- Where can I apply an inventive solution instead of relying on familiar methods?
- What constraints could become catalysts for innovation if reframed intentionally?
- Who outside my immediate circle should be part of my next strategic conversation?
- What partnership could unlock exponential value not just incremental benefit?
- Who benefits from my leadership today and who should benefit tomorrow?

- How will I ensure that my influence uplifts more people than it protects?
- Where do we hesitate when courage is required?
- Are we still learning at the speed the world demands?
- Do we collaborate deeply—or just coordinate politely?
- Who benefits from our leadership beyond shareholders?
- What leadership legacy are we actively shaping?

Closing Note

This appendix is not meant to be completed once. It is meant to be revisited.

The boards and leaders who endure are not those with perfect answers but those who return, again and again, to the right questions.

Appendix B — Board Reflection Checklist (One-Page Tool)

Use quarterly or annually

Governance Readiness

- ❑ AI systems mapped and tiered by risk
- ❑ Clear accountability for AI outcomes
- ❑ Ethics embedded into operations

Speed & Discipline

- ❑ Decisions matched to appropriate cadence
- ❑ Guardrails enable experimentation
- ❑ Resilience built intentionally

Global & Cultural Intelligence

- ❑ Board includes global perspective
- ❑ Strategies tested across regions
- ❑ Technology adapted to local context

Leadership & Trust

- ❑ Board learning plan in place
- ❑ Trust metrics reviewed regularly
- ❑ Service and stewardship discussed

Appendix C — Board Offsite Agenda Using the Reflection Questions

Board Offsite: Governing the Future

Duration: 1 day (or 2 half-days)

Session 1 — The World Has Changed (90 min)

- Reflection questions from Chapters 1, 5, 7
- AI, risk, accountability discussion
- Identify top 3 governance gaps

Session 2 — Speed vs. Resilience (75 min)

- Chapters 2, 3, 4 reflections
- Where speed helps / where it hurts
- Redesign one decision pathway

Session 3 — Global Reality Check (75 min)

- Chapters 8, 9 reflections
- Cultural, regulatory blind spots
- Stress-test one global assumption

Session 4 — Board of the Future (90 min)

- Chapters 10–13 reflections
- Skills, composition, learning gaps
- Create a 12-month board evolution roadmap

Closing Reflection

- What must change in the next 90 days?

- What legacy are we choosing?
- Are we governing the future—or reacting to it?

Final Note

This appendix is intentionally demanding.
Boards that use it once will learn something.
Boards that return to it regularly will transform.

Appendix D — Agility Transfer Model (ATM)

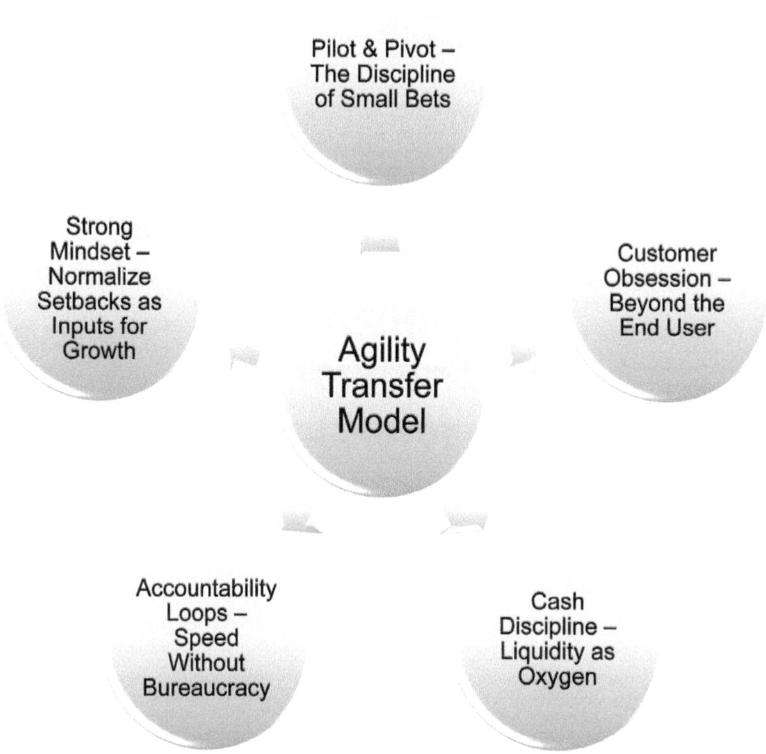

Appendix E — Resilience Transfer Model (RTM)

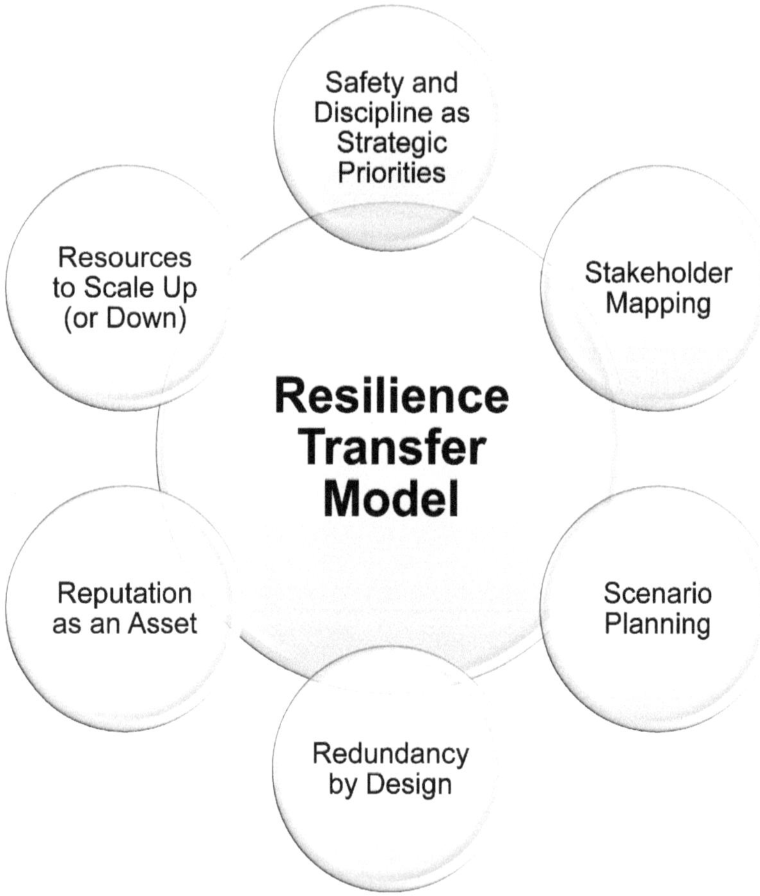

Appendix F — Accountable AI

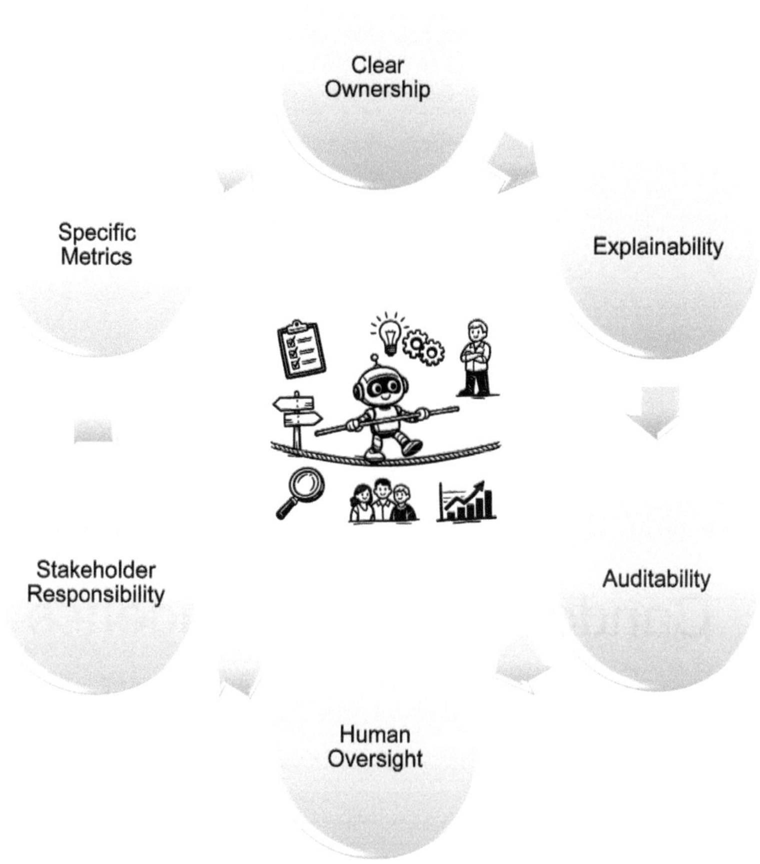

Appendix G - The Right-Sized Governance Compass

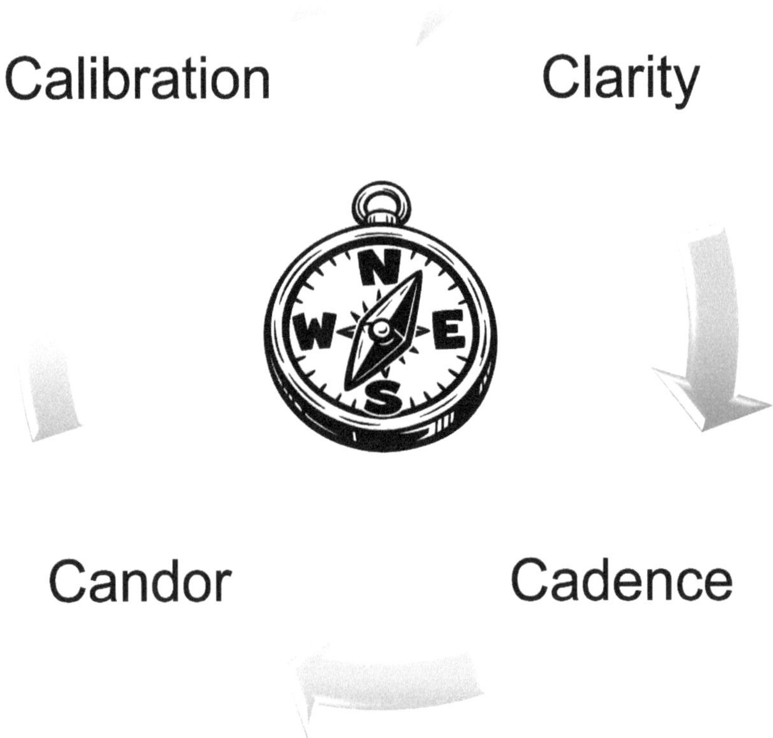

Appendix H - Boardroom Risk Compass

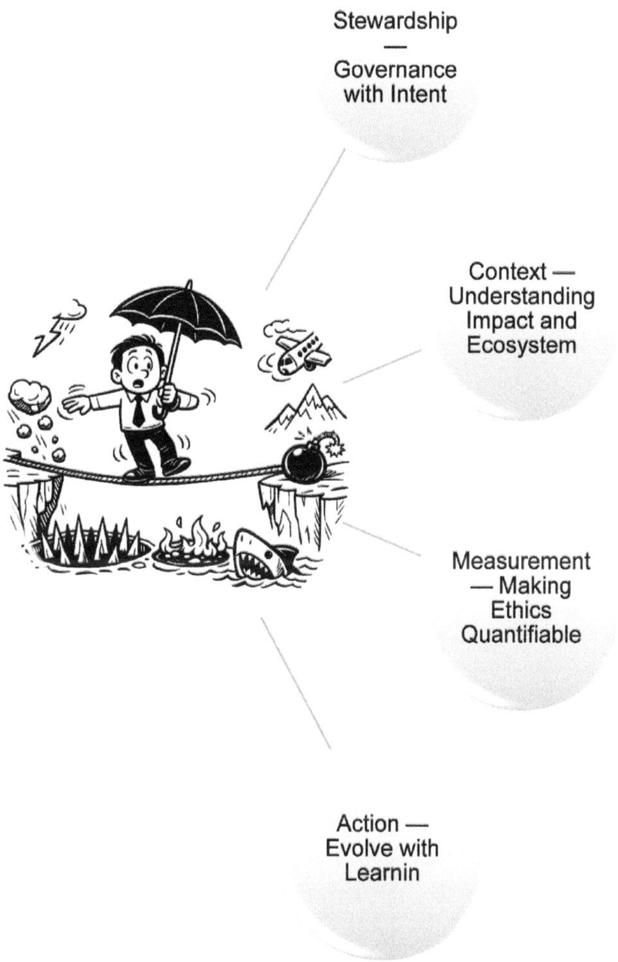

Author's Note

This book was shaped by nearly three decades spent moving between boardrooms, operating roles, startups, and global organizations, often at moments of disruption. My career has crossed legacy industries such as energy and franchising, entrepreneurial ventures built from the ground up, and technology and AI-focused companies navigating scale, risk, and trust. Along the way, I've served as a board director, advisor, executive, and founder, working across five continents and with organizations at very different stages of maturity. What connects all those experiences is a single, recurring tension: governance systems designed for yesterday struggling to guide decisions that define tomorrow.

I did not write this book as an academic exercise, nor as a definitive manual. I wrote it as a practitioner, someone who has seen governance work well, fail quietly, and sometimes fail publicly. Many of the questions in these chapters are the same ones I use in my own board work. In fact, while writing this book, I shared several of these reflection questions with fellow directors, founders and investors to spark discussion. The response was consistent: the value wasn't in having the "right" answer, but in finally asking the right questions together. If this book helps you generate even a handful of deeper, more honest conversations in your boardroom or leadership team, it has done its job.

I see this work as part of an ongoing dialogue. Governance, leadership, global activities and technology will continue to evolve and so must our thinking. I welcome your feedback, reflections, disagreements, and stories from the field. You can learn more about some of my work or reach me directly at https://www.fdaisolutions.com/boardingthefuture. I read every message. If this book challenged your assumptions, helped you rethink your governance model, or prompted a conversation that mattered, I'd genuinely like to hear about it.

Thank you for engaging deeply with these ideas and for doing the hard work of governing the future, not the past.

www.ingramcontent.com/pod-product-compliance
Ingram Content Group UK Ltd.
Pitfield, Milton Keynes, MK11 3LW, UK
UKHW040228290926
15471UKWH00001B/56

9 781946 637499